Heart

of a Woman

Sparkling inspiration and insights
on the strength and wisdom of women

Sheryl L. Roush

SPARKLE PRESS
SAN DIEGO, CALIFORNIA

Published by Sparkle Press
A division of Sparkle Presentations
Post Office Box 2373, La Mesa, California 91943 USA

Send contributions to Sheryl@SparklePresentations.com

Visit our website at: www.SparklePresentations.com

First Printing April 2007

Library of Congress Cataloging-in-Publication Data
Roush, Sheryl Lynn.
Heart of a Woman
Sparkling inspiration and insights
on the strength and wisdom of women/Sheryl L. Roush
ISBN 10: 1-88087-813-5
ISBN 13: 978-1-88087-813-2

1. Self-Help   2. Inspirational   3. Women's Issues

Printed in Canada.

Heart of a Woman

The heart of a woman is like a great big purse.
It can contain the entire universe.
There is room for friends and long lost lovers,
For dogs and kittens, fathers and mothers.
And in the core is the place for boys and girls,
For their bright eyes and shining curls.
They are our futures and our legacy
Our proud achievement that anyone can see.
Yes, in the heart of a woman, there are many things,
The ability to love, and laugh and to give up dreams.
Like that old purse, sometimes tattered and sore
A woman's heart can always stretch to hold a little more.

~ ROSALIE FERRER KRAMER

WOMAN

A woman is a wondrous, magnificent creature,
a princess, a goddess, a queen.
She is worthy of, and deserves,
love, adoration and respect.
She is a mystical creature
blessed and guided by an inner knowing
of what is right and true.
She gives life and nurtures it ever so gently
with tenderness and love.
Her spirit is playful and passionate,
Her movement fluid and graceful.
Her strength lies in her knowledge of self
as she moves forward freely, confidently,
caressing life with gentleness and greatness.
Allowing love to flood her heart, she heals with her feminine touch
and give birth to things divine
She speaks not in anger but centers herself in truth
and uses the power of her voice to soothe,
speaking calmly, clearly, compassionately
for the highest good of all concerned.
She is magnetic, regal and wise.
She carries her head held high.
She has an inner light, a spiritual essence
that, when revealed,
is so enchanting, so captivating, so alluring
that all who experience, this vision of loveliness,
find that they are drawn to her
with the intense desire to know
her secrets of beauty, wisdom and peace.

~ CATHERINE TILLEY

From My Heart to Yours

*T*his book is dedicated to "Heart of a Woman"—that soulful essence, the passionate being that keeps harmony, offers solace, forgiveness and maternal gracious love from every cell of its Being!

We are daughters, sisters, aunts, cousins, mothers, grandmothers, great grandmothers, friends, chosen family and above all—Goddesses!

When I think of what it means to be a woman today—and the opportunities available to us—it's amazing! The choices are, and always have been—up to us! I look to the life of my grandmother, who raised seven kids during the Depression on a dairy farm in Iowa. I see her as a woman of fortitude, perseverance, limitless love and inner strength! She worked her fingers to the bone, and still found time for prayers, kittens, and granddaughters.

Thank you to those who have inspired and encouraged me on my path to authenticity and understanding my own worthiness over these growing years. The journey has been abundantly filled with challenges and character-building experiences, none of which would I change. To the women in my life who have graciously served as role models of assertiveness, spirituality and authenticity—I thank you. To the men in my life who have uniquely served me—to further comprehend and embrace my genuineness and feminine spirit—I thank you as well. I have grown to be who I am today because of you. For the lessons of strength with softness, fortitude with grace, confidence with calm, Divine surrender from controlling drive, inner knowing with inner peace, trust and worthiness, and above all, love—I thank you.

With abundant appreciation I acknowledge my numerous cherished friends, and mentors: God, Gloria Boileau, Lisa Delman, Linda Lou Ferber, Debbi McGill, Sandy Liarakos, Mary Marcdante, Catherine Tilley, Beverly Weurding, and oh yes—Oprah Winfrey.

From My Heart to Yours,

Sheryl

FOREWORD

*I*t was another warm moonlit evening in Southern California. I had just finished giving a presentation at an upscale resort on how to be the star you are when my cell phone rang. "Cynthia, please come to our ladies impromptu celebration. There are some fabulous women I want you to meet," my new friend exclaimed. I was tired and not really anxious to make the 50-mile jaunt in bottleneck traffic. My female intuition told me to go so I hopped in my rental car to frolic in feminine fun.

The moment I walked in the door, I saw her. There she was—all sparkles, sprinkles, and stars—Sheryl Roush! I knew instantly that I wanted to meet this passionate lady. Sheryl is the type of woman that you instantly adore—she is bubbly, inclusive, and, well, she sparkles. I have always been known as "The Star Lady" and standing next to me was the "Sparkle-Tude" expert. What a great combo. A fellow cheer-leader for positive attitudes!

The book you are holding in your hands is a tribute to the huge heart of Sheryl Roush and her dedication to empowering women and the world at large through love. In our society, women tend to be the caregivers, the heart of the home, the backbone of the family. We are mothers, wives, daughters, sisters, aunts, friends, partners, colleagues, and lovers. We all share the desire to love and be loved. Sheryl shows us the way to love abundantly every day in every way with the wealth of words in this thoughtful treasure.

I was fortunate to come from a family where my parents loved and worshiped one another. My parents believed that fathers and mothers were equal partners with different but very complimentary roles. Because of their caring relationship with one another, we were shown a superb example of how males and females can relate to each other. As a result, we developed rich, respectful relationships with both genders. The love of husband for wife and wife for husband is the greatest gift parents can bequeath to their offspring. When children witness the devotion of their parents to one another, they feel safe, comforted, and loved. They grow up to love and be loved. To be a great parent, we must first love our self, then love our partner. Together we love our children.

To have a friend, you must first be a friend. So it is with love. Love is not a competition. We must give love freely and be willing to open our spirits to let love flow to us. When we love with our souls, love fills our hearts. Love is not always easy. Love hurts. Love is getting our hands dirty and bruised to make sure the ones we care for feel supported, believed, and encouraged to be the stars of their own lives. Love is patient, honest, real, and kind. Love is leading with your heart, not with your head.

I am grateful that I made the journey to San Diego that evening as I met a great guide. As the song says, "What the world needs now, is love sweet love. It's the only thing that there's just too little of." Sheryl offers sparkling inspiration to you, too, with this publication. She has compiled the most incredible quotes, poems, anecdotes, stories, and tips to help you love more fully right now. Indulge in her warmth. Accept her gifts. Be a beacon for love.

You are a shining star. Start sparkling because *love* is you.

Starstyle® blessings,

Be the Star You Are!

Cynthia Brian

www.star-style.com
www.bethestaryouare.org

Contents

Ageless Living 1
Angels 5
Art 7
Authenticity & Uniqueness 8
A Woman's Intuition 12
A Woman's Wisdom 13
Babies 15
Being a Mother 17
Cats 18
Challenges 20
Children 22
Chocolate 26
Choice & Common Sense 27
Communication 28
Count Your Blessings 30
Courage 31
Dance 39
Dating 41
Daughters 43
Death & Grieving 48
Do It Anyway 58
Dogs 59
Dreams 61
Estrogen 62
Faith 63
Falling in Love 64
Family 66
Fathers 69
Finding Love 74
Forgiveness 79

Flowers & Gardens 80
Friendship 84
Fulfill Your Heart's Desire 87
God 88
Grandfathers 91
Grandmothers 94
Gratitude & Happiness 100
Health 101
Heart 106
Heartache & Heartbreak 107
Hobbies 111
Hugs 112
Husbands 113
In Sickness & In Health 117
Kindness 118
Kisses 121
Laughter 123
Learning to Love Yourself 124
Let Me Call You Sweetheart 130
Letting Go of Anger 135
Life 138
Living with Joy 143
Love 146
Love Lost 160
Making a Difference 163
Marriage 166
Men! 174
Mentoring 182
Mid-Life for Women 183

Military Relationships 184
Mothers 185
Music 195
Nature 197
Old Maid Next Door 198
Parenting 199
Passion 204
Patriotism 207
Pets 210
Prayer 212
Pregnancy 216
Prosperity 218
Prosperity CONTINUED 219
Raising Fearless Women 220
Re-Awakening to Love 228
Relationships 230
Romance 238
Self 242
Sisters 250
Sons 257
Sparkle-Tude Boosters 259
Stay at Home Moms 261
Teenagers 263
Trust 264
Unconditional Support 266
Women 267
Women in History 268
Worthiness 271

◆ ◆ ◆

Author Information 275

Ageless Living

HOW TO STAY YOUNG
Throw out nonessential numbers.
This includes age, weight and height.
Let the doctor worry about them. That is why you pay him/her.

Keep only cheerful friends. The grouches pull you down.

Keep learning. Learn more about the computer, crafts, gardening, whatever. Never let the brain idle.

Enjoy the simple things.

Laugh often, long and loud. Laugh until you gasp for breath.

The tears happen. Endure, grieve, and move on.
The only person who is with us our entire life, is God.
Be *alive* while you are alive.

Surround yourself with what you love, whether it's family, pets, keepsakes, music, plants, hobbies, whatever. Your home is your refuge.

Cherish your health: If it is good, preserve it. If it is unstable, improve it. If it is beyond what you can improve, get help.

Don't take guilt trips. Take a trip to the mall, to the next county, to a foreign country, but *not* to where the guilt is.

Tell the people you love that you love them, at every opportunity.
~ AUTHOR OF UNKNOWN

Ageless Living

You never grow old until you've lost all your marvels.
~ MERRY BROWNE

Few women admit their age . . .
Fewer men act theirs.
~ BUMPER STICKER

The woman who tells her age is either too young to have anything to lose or too old to have anything to gain.
~ CHINESE PROVERB

Gray hair is God's graffiti.
~ BILL COSBY

The really frightening thing about middle age is the knowledge that you'll grow out of it.
~ DORIS DAY

One of the many things nobody ever tells you about middle age is that it's such a nice change from being young.
~ DOROTHY CANFIELD FISHER

The years that a woman subtracts from her age are not lost. They are added to other women's.
~ DIANE DE POITIERS

Middle Age is when your age starts to show around your middle.
~ BOB HOPE

Ageless Living CONTINUED

Make time for young people—you are their role models.
Make time for old people—they need to know you care.
One day, to too, will be old.
Make time for you so that your time with others
will be enriched by the love you give to yourself.

~ SANDRA SCHRIFT
Career Coach, www.schrift.com

Dear Lord if I have to be this way,
Please take me now I cannot stay.
I can't recall what I said yesterday,
I dread repeating it anyway.
And don't let me stay so long a while,
That I have to fake another smile,
When the packer in the grocery store,
Inquires if I need his help once more
Alas that phone's ringing off the hook.
My granddaughter says she's learning to cook,
And that her first baby is on the way,
So please Dear Lord don't take me TODAY!
Now I want to stay on my sojourn,
Until my new great-grandchild is born.
And maybe until there'll be another,
Who can also call me great-grandmother
Old age isn't perfect but it's never a bore,
'Specially with new little ones to adore.
And so, Dear Lord, I pray you'll ignore
All that dumb stuff I told you before.

~ ROSALIE FERRER KRAMER
Speaker, poet, author of Senior Humor, *www.authorsden.com/rosaliefkramer*

ODE TO MY WAIST AND TO THE WAITRESS
You stand there with pad and pencil,
pert little pears glaring, blinding me,
mocking my own gravity-laden appendages
now sliding like melting glaciers
into the muddy sea of my hips.

You flaunt by not hiding
that wasp-waist of yours,
an affront to thick middles the world over,
tight thighs taunting, singsong, I can hear them:
"We don't need control-tops."

Two words:
just wait.

~ LYNN MARSHALL GAHMAN

Angels

Don't forget to be kind to strangers. For some who have done this have entertained angels without realizing it.

~ HEBREWS 13:2

Be like an angel and do one small act of service for someone; be a blessing in someone's life. We are building a bridge according to God's will and plan. Look around your community with "Angel Eyes" filled with God's light—to see where service is needed and know that God has sent you. Spread the positive and uplifting light of your spirit. Open your heart and mind to your intuitive side and feel the healing power of unconditional love that exists all around. We are here to serve God—Just like angels.

~ JAYNE HOWARD-FELDMAN

Angels do find us in our hour of need.

~ AMY HUFFMAN

I was on my way to a Christmas celebration during a horrible rainstorm. My little Miata hydroplaned across the freeway while I was struck hard four times. Landing in the center divider, I bled from wounds to my head, bled internally from my spleen, and had problems breathing due to seven broken ribs. A woman, Maureen, stopped her car with her two toddlers in tow to give me assistance. She called 911, located my wife on my cell phone to inform her of what happened, and stayed with me until paramedics arrived. I never saw or heard from her again but she helped calm and assure me. My wife and I call her our angel and know that this special person is given divine guidance and protection.

~ MARSHALL L. LIGHTNER, PHD

Angels CONTINUED

*M*y daughter Rose, two years old, and I sleep in the same bed. Recently I have been witnessing some unusual and interesting interactions between her and what I think are her angels. I like to listen to the soundtrack, "In Search of Angels" before bed. It always gives me chills and I think the angels like it.

One night my daughter jumps up in bed and starts singing along, but her eyes swam back and forth in the dark and she was laughing, like she was watching something flying. I got quiet and watched her for a while. She had her head tilted back and was making like little dog paddling swimming motions (something she had never done before), twirling her arms around in circles making flying motions with her hands. I asked, "Are you seeing angels?" She grinned and nodded her head. "Where are the angels?" She pointed to the ceiling, "Up high." I asked her, "What do the angels do?" She just grinned and made more paddling motions with her arms. I took her to a bookstore, showed her an angel art book. She didn't respond, until we got to a picture of Mary surrounded by flying cherubs, then she shrieked, "Angels!"

She has seen a picture of the Virgin Mary's face and shrieked "Angel!" I don't know if she has seen her before or not, or mistook her for an angel. I also heard her talking in the dark for a long time.

I don't question these incidents, but I do find them comforting.

I believe children see things adults don't see. Once when I was young, I was scared to sleep and I prayed for angels to be with me. When I woke up, I saw golden hair quivering just over the edge of my bed. My eyes were wide open, and I wasn't dreaming. I leaned over the side of the bed and saw a child about three foot tall. It turned around, and it had a cherubim face and blue eyes. I don't recall wings. In a second it was gone. When my daughter does these things I wonder if she is seeing an angel like I saw when I was very young.

~ CHRISSY HURLEY

Art

Life beats down and crushes the soul and art reminds you that you have one.
~ STELLA ADLER

All great art comes from a sense of outrage.
~ GLENN CLOSE

Art is the desire of a man to express himself, to record the reactions of his personality to the world he lives in.
~ AMY LOWELL

Art is the colors and textures of your imagination.
~ MEGHAN, LOS CERROS MIDDLE SCHOOL

I found I could say things with color and shapes that I couldn't say any other way—things I had no words for.
~ GEORGIA O'KEEFFE

Anyone who says you can't see a thought simply doesn't know art.
~ WYNETKA ANN REYNOLDS

Art is your personal diary where you may color your thoughts and emotions on a page.
~ SARA, LOS CERROS MIDDLE SCHOOL

Art is a shadow of what a person is thinking . . . a small glimpse of what they hold inside. Little secrets, regrets, joys . . . every line has its own meaning.
~ SARAH, LOS CERROS MIDDLE SCHOOL

Authenticity & Uniqueness

Doubt who you will, but never yourself.
~ CHRISTINE BOVEE

Why compare yourself with others? No one in the entire world can do a better job of being you than you.
~ SUSAN CARLSON

It's amazing how many cares disappear when one decides not to be something, but to be someone.
~ COCO CHANEL

We need to find the courage to say NO to the things and people that are not serving us if we want to rediscover ourselves and live our lives with authenticity.
~ BARBARA DE ANGELIS

Always be a first-rate version of yourself, instead of a second-rate version of somebody else.
~ JUDY GARLAND

You are unique, and if that is not fulfilled, then something wonderful has been lost.
~ MARTHA GRAHAM

The most exhausting thing in life is being insincere.
~ ANNE MORROW LINDBERGH

Be courageous. It's one of the only places left uncrowded.
~ ANITA RODDICK

Authenticity & Uniqueness continued

Your Authentic Self—

Identity

*R*oots, neurotic roots form a recognition deep, form a familiar face, claiming a familiar path, etched in the pathways of my brain.

So distant they are from the passion of vision that seeps into the waking. Like a dream that slowly penetrates the consciousness on its way to taking over.

In the interim of this taking over, is a bodiless consciousness, observing, witnessing, feeling. Feeling, yes feeling deeply, the presence of those comprising my outer world. So strongly felt is the experience, the neurotic self fades back and back.

And bigger and bigger the passion of the vision grows, and demands a presence in me to carry it into full view. Neurosis, unfit as a vessel, will not do. And the invisible witness serves no more.

Out of what matter will this presence be created? Where are the roots and foundation of genuineness to create this being, who has never before stood on earth? Born of piercing intention, one-pointed, yet rich and full, pounding into my brain and heart and being. Intention born of the pulsating passion of the vision, bursting out of my yearning heart, births the powerful, sensual, sexual presence, larger than the physical stature of the human woman.

Authenticity & Uniqueness

Born of unflinching vision, unafraid of truth's essence hidden in the unknown, she leaps out into the world in joyous truth and love, uncovering the magical reality under the surface. Taking up expansive space, with each step opening up vast new worlds, blessed in her triumphal majesty.

And so I stand in awe of this new being, destined to be me.

Who shall say the human soul is not the vehicle for the essence of the Divine?

~ JANE ILENE COHEN
Spiritually-based, transformational counselor, teacher and visionary, www.janecohen.net
© Copyright 2004

What lies behind us and what lies before us are are tiny matters compared to what lies within us.
~ RALPH WALDO EMERSON

While we have the gift of life, it seems to me the only tragedy is to allow part of us to die—whether it is our spirit, our creativity or our glorious uniqueness.
~ GILDA RADNER

Our childlike self is the deepest level of our being.
~ MARIANNE WILLIAMSON
Speaker, author of Return to Love

Authenticity & Uniqueness <small>CONTINUED</small>

LIVING AN AUTHENTIC LIFE

*L*iving authentically is the most important aspect of living soulfully. There is nothing more important or meaningful in life than honoring your authentic self—your true nature—and expressing it in the world. When you honor your most authentic self—your Spirit—you are allowing your Light to shine and touch the world. Living authentically, in its simplest terms, is living your Truth, the truth in your heart and soul.

It's allowing yourself to be guided by Divine Truth and Wisdom, each and every day, and doing your Highest, most authentic work in the world. It's joyfully creating and living your Highest purpose!

Living authentically is not always easy. It can be hard work, but the rewards are worth the effort. It requires the courage to ask yourself the hard questions and be completely honest with yourself about what is truly important to you in life and how you can live your Highest Good. It's following your heart's wisdom, living your Truth, and being real in every sense.

When you are living an authentic life, you are contributing your soulful nature and gifts to the world and, thus, creating a better, more authentic and soulful life experience for us all.

~ VALERIE RICKEL
Founder and Soul, www.SoulfulLiving.com

A Woman's Intuition

Trust your hunches. They're usually based on facts filed away just below the conscious level.

~ DR. JOYCE BROTHERS
Psychologist and Television Personality

Every time you don't follow your inner guidance, you feel a loss of energy, loss of power, a sense of spiritual deadness.

~ SHAKTI GAWAIN

Hunch. Gut feeling. Voice of God. Instinct. Many names. One Force.

~ CATH KACHUR
Speaker, artist, www.HumanTuneUp.com

Women don't listen to the voice inside them. We get our lives so busy—it [intuition] is a gift from God.

~ MARIE OSMOND, ON *OPRAH*

Listen to your intuition, for it is your best friend, ignore your fears, for they are your enemy, believe in your dreams, for they are your future.

~ BARBARA SANFILIPPO
Speaker, author of Dream Big! What's the Best That Can Happen, *www.Barbara-Sanfilippo.com*

From the moment Eve took a bite of that fruit from the tree in the middle of the garden, just as she was promised, her eyes were opened and she did indeed gain the knowledge of good and evil. It's called women's intuition and it has been passed down from generation to generation for thousands of years. In some cultures it is revered, in others condemned and feared. But one thing has remained constant down through the decades—every woman knows that she has it.

~ JONI WILSON
Speaker, singer, voice expert, authorJoniWilsonVoice.com © 2005 Joni Wilson. All Rights Reserved. Reprinted with Permission. From Thunder Behind the Silence: When a Woman Finds Her Voice

A Woman's Wisdom

In every girl is a goddess.
~ FRANCESCA LIA BLOCK

Women are never what they seem to be. There is the woman you see and there is the woman who is hidden. Buy the gift for the woman who is hidden.
~ ERMA BOMBECK

See yourself in everything because everything is already within you.
~ CYNTHIA BRIAN
Speaker, author of the New York Times *best-selling* Chicken Soup for the Gardener's Soul, Be the Star You Are!, The Business of Show Business *and others. www.star-style.com*

The flower of a woman's wisdom blooms within her heart.
~ LAUREL BURCH
Artist Celebrating the Heart of Womankind

Never mistake knowledge for wisdom. One helps you make a living; the other helps you make a life.
~ SANDRA CAREY

There is space within sisterhood for likeness and difference, for the subtle differences that challenge and delight; there is space for disappointment—and surprise.
~ CHRISTINE DOWNING

God gave women intuition and femininity. Used properly, the combination easily jumbles the brain of any man I've ever met.
~ FARRAH FAWCETT

A Woman's Wisdom

I used to tell my children "Do well, stay well." Then the youngest changed it to "Be well, stay well" and we both grew up.

~ LINDA FERBER

Don't compromise yourself. You are all you've got.

~ JANIS JOPLIN

A woman is the full circle. Within her is the power to create, nurture, and transform.

~ DIANE MARIECHILD

Wisdom is not knowing what to do, it is knowing what Not to do.

~ STEPHANIE MOLES
www.TheWoman'sHeart.org

How wrong it is for a woman to expect the man to build the world she wants, rather than to create it herself.

~ ANAIS NIN

I am a woman above everything else.

~ JACQUELINE BOUVIER KENNEDY ONASSIS

Life on the planet is born of woman.

~ ADRIENNE RICH

You gain strength, courage and confidence by every experience in which you really stop to look fear in the face. You are able to say to yourself, "I lived through this horror. I can take the next thing that comes along." . . . You must do the thing you think you cannot do.

~ ELEANOR ROOSEVELT

Babies

CHERUB

Cherub you are, with little
porcelain hand wrapped
around extended finger.
Eyelashes cover virgin eyes
to a world in which I shelter you—
You are still an innocent
as sweet as the pink blossom
on your newly formed lips.
Perfect are your features,
and pore less is your skin.
Did you fall from heaven—
my precious white winged angel?
Where do you hide your wings?
I swaddle you in Mother's arms
never wanting this moment's end.

~ LEE A. BARRON, PUBLISHER, AUTHOR
Copyright © 2004 Lee A. Barron

Father asked us what was God's noblest work.
Anna said men, but I said babies.
Men are often bad, but babies never are.

~ LOUISA MAY ALCOTT

Giving birth is like taking your lower lip and forcing it over your head.

~ CAROL BURNETT

It was the tiniest thing I ever decided to put my whole life into.

~ TERRI GUILLEMETS

Babies CONTINUED

A woman has two smiles that an angel might envy—the smile that accepts a lover before words are uttered, and the smile that lights on the first born babe, and assures it of a mother's love.

~ THOMAS C. HALIBURTON

Babies are necessary to grown-ups. A new baby is like the beginning of all things wonder, hope, a dream of possibilities. In a world that is cutting down its trees to build highways, losing its earth to concrete . . . babies are almost the only remaining link with nature, with the natural world of living things from which we spring.

~ EDA J. LE SHAN

My obstetrician was so dumb that when I gave birth he forgot to cut the cord. For a year that kid followed me everywhere. It was like having a dog on a leash.

~ JOAN RIVERS

A baby is God's opinion that the world should go on.

~ CARL SANDBURG

It sometimes happens, even in the best of families, that a baby is born. This is not necessarily cause for alarm. The important thing is to keep your wits about you and borrow some money.

~ ELINOR GOULDING SMITH

A baby is an angel whose wings decrease as his legs increase.

~ UNKNOWN

On a Maternity Room door:
"Push. Push. Push."

Being a Mother

*B*eing a mother is the most important, yet under-rated job that I'll ever have. No amount of money, no prestige or grand title that anyone could bestow upon me, is more valuable than to hear my little girl say that she loves me when I tuck her in.

Everything I do is for the benefit of her and my husband. I never thought I could be so unselfish with my time, energy, and affection. But here I am, four years after getting married, and almost that long since I learned that I was blessed to be pregnant at 43. Although I was in very good health and physical condition, we were so worried that there might be something "not right," due to my age. But she was "perfect."

I endured nine months of chronic nausea, frequent discomfort (including an extremely long amniocentesis needle, not to mention the sore back, hips and feet or the scar from the C-section), regular schedule changes, and an enormous amount of fatigue. Yet, I would do it all over again in a heartbeat for another child.

I held her to my breast and nursed her for 5 months. I still rock her to sleep at night, even though she's old enough to get into bed by herself at this point. I taught her to pray before meals, play nicely, say "please" and "thank you," be patient (do you have any idea how difficult it is for a 2-year-old to wait, even for a minute), to eat with a fork and spoon, to love the outdoors, the difference between a bathtub and a pool, to sing "Happy Birthday," and so much more. She absorbed all of it, and is now a beautiful, happy, articulate, opinionated 3-year-old.

It's difficult not to spoil her. However, I know that to grow into a loving, confident adult, she needs discipline tempered with love; safety and security couched in exploration; answers surrounded by more questions; and faith nestled in tolerance. I have only a short time to give her all of this, and I will spend every waking moment being her mother. It's an awesome responsibility, one that I take seriously and eagerly.

~ SHARON M. MCCARTHY, MEGAN'S MOM

Cats

1. Always be ready to play.
2. When you are happy to see someone, stretch your arms up to them and ask to be picked up.
3. If the person you love forgets to feed you dinner, don't take it personally.
4. Talk to the one you love, incessantly and constantly.
5. Don't be afraid to ask to be touched.
6. Show your love and adoration by bringing presents.
7. Purr when the person you love is anywhere near you.
8. Encourage the person you love to take naps with you.
9. Always comfort the person you love, regardless of whether they need emotional or physical comfort.

~ UNKNOWN

In the middle of a world that has always been a bit mad, the cat walks with confidence.

~ ROSEANNE ANDERSON

The cat is above all things, a dramatist.

~ MARGARET BENSON

Dogs come when they're called; cats take a message and get back to you later.

~ MARY BLY

Who among us hasn't envied a cat's ability to ignore the cares of daily life and to relax completely?

~ KAREN BRADEMEYER

Cats continued

Our perfect companions never have fewer than four feet.
~ COLETTE

If there were to be a universal sound depicting peace, I would surely vote for the purr.
~ BARBARA L. DIAMOND

Purring would seem to be, in her case, an automatic safety valve device for dealing with happiness overflow.
~ MONICA EDWARDS

A cat is a puzzle for which there is no solution.
~ HAZEL NICHOLSON

There is no snooze button on a cat that wants breakfast.
~ UNKNOWN

It is impossible to keep a straight face in the presence of one or more kittens.
~ CYNTHIA E. VARNADO

Dogs have masters. Cats have staff.
~ UNKNOWN

Dogs believe they are human.
Cats believe they are God.
~ UNKNOWN

Challenges

Bouncing Back from Life's Setbacks

Create an action plan that will move you through the madness and bounce back from the rough roads that lie ahead.

1. Reinforce The Belief In Yourself
2. Assess The Impact Of Your Crisis
3. Understand What You Can And Cannot Control
4. Call On Your Inner Strength
5. Talk To Others
6. Don't Lose Your Sense Of Humor
7. Bounce Back

~ CAROLE COPELAND THOMAS, MBA
Speaker, www.TellCarole.com

You don't develop courage by being happy in your relationships everyday. You develop it by surviving difficult times and challenging adversity.

~ BARBARA DE ANGELIS

Blessed are the flexible for they shall not be bent out of shape.

~ CATH KACHUR
Speaker, artist

Pain is not a punishment. Pain is a gift. It's an invitation to *grow*. Our difficulties call us to go deeper within ourselves. Our challenges force us to develop better skills and new ways of thinking, doing and being. They draw forth a greater strength and wisdom from our inner selves.

~ PEGGY O'NEILL
Speaker, author of Walking Tall: Overcoming Inner Smallness No Matter What Size You Are, *www.YoPeggy.com*

Challenges CONTINUED

No matter how much you're struggling today, always look to tomorrow. Then you will look back and realize you can always, manage whatever life brings you.
~ JOANNE ROUSH

Every blade of grass has its angel that bends over it and whispers, grow, grow.
~ *THE TALMUD*

Challenges make you discover things about yourself that you never really knew.
~ CICELY TYSON

The difference between stumbling blocks and stepping stones is how you use them.
~ UNKNOWN

Always continue the climb. It is possible for you to do whatever you choose, if you first get to know who you are and are willing to work with a power that is greater than ourselves to do it.
~ OPRAH WINFREY

Children

THE QUIET HOUR
Around four o'clock it sneaks up on me,
The silence is not as it used to be.
Once there was a noisy bunch,
TV's a stereo all playing at once.
Bickering, laughter, a good cooking smell,
Mother is home so all is well.
They're gone today but it's in my power,
To bring them back, in the quiet hour.
Listening carefully, I hear them now.
Sounds of my children, but I know not how.

~ ROSALIE FERRER KRAMER
Speaker, poet, author of Dancing in the Dark: Things My Mother Never Told Me
www.authorsden.com/rosaliefkramer

Children's talent to endure stems from their ignorance of alternatives.

~ MAYA ANGELOU
Author of I Know Why the Caged Bird Sings, *1969*

Children are like flowers, nurture them and they will grow up strong
and beautiful.

~ LYDIA BOYD
Past International Director, Toastmasters International

If our American way of life fails the child, it fails us all.

~ PEARL S. BUCK

It always cracks me up that mothers will tell their children to say "no"
to their peers when they can't say "no" themselves.

~ COLETTE CARLSON
Speaker, contributing author of Conversations on Success www.colettecarlson.com

Children CONTINUED

A child's world is fresh and new and beautiful, full of wonder and excitement. It is our misfortune that for most of us that clear-eyed vision, that true instinct for what is beautiful and awe-inspiring, is dimmed and even lost before we reach adulthood.
~ RACHEL CARSON

Cleaning your house while your kids are still growing up is like shoveling the walk before it stops snowing.
~ PHYLLIS DILLER

Life, love, and laughter—what priceless gifts to give our children.
~ PHYLLIS DRYDEN

There was never a child so lovely but his mother was glad to get him to sleep.
~ RALPH WALDO EMERSON

Parents can only give good advice or put [their children] on the right paths, but the final forming of a person's character lies in their own hands.
~ ANNE FRANK

I believe that children are our future.
Teach them well and let them lead the way.
Show them all the beauty they possess inside.
~ WHITNEY HOUSTON
Mother, singer, actress

Children

Think what a better world it would be if we all, the whole world, had cookies and milk about three o'clock every afternoon and then lay down on our blankets for a nap.

~ BARBARA JORDAN

The real menace in dealing with a five-year-old is that in no time at all you begin to sound like a five-year-old.

~ JOAN KERR
Please Don't Eat the Daisies, *1957*

Children are contemptuous, haughty, irritable, envious, sneaky, self-ish, lazy, flighty, timid, liars and hypocrites, quick to laugh and cry, extreme in expressing joy and sorrow, especially about trifles, they'll do anything to avoid pain but they enjoy inflicting it: little men already.

~ JEAN DE LA BRUYÈRE
Les Caractères, *1688*

Women gather together to wear silly hats, eat dainty food, and forget how unresponsive their husbands are. Men gather to talk sports, eat heavy food, and forget how demanding their wives are. Only where children gather is there any real chance of fun.

~ MIGNON MCLAUGHLIN

Children are one third of our population and all of our future.

~ SELECT PANEL FOR THE PROMOTION OF CHILD HEALTH, 1981

Children desperately need to know—and to hear in ways they under-stand and remember—that they're loved and valued by mom and dad.

~ PAUL SMALLY

Children CONTINUED

Parents learn a lot from their children about coping with life.
~ MURIEL SPARK

Each day of our lives we make deposits in the memory banks of our children.
~ CHARLES R. SWINDOLL

We worry about what a child will become tomorrow, yet we forget that (s)he is someone today.
~ STACIA TAUSCHER

Little children look right through that which we have learned to be and into the beauty of our soul. This is truly love.
~ CATHERINE TILLEY
Founder of the Institute for Global Healing and Publisher of WISE Publications
www.theglobalvoice.com

If you have a lot of tension and you get a headache, do what it says on the aspirin bottle: "Take two aspirin" and "Keep away from children."
~ UNKNOWN

A child can ask questions that a wise man cannot answer.
~ UNKNOWN

Children seldom misquote. In fact, they usually repeat word for word what you shouldn't have said.
~ UNKNOWN

Children are the living messages we send to a time we will not see.
~ JOHN W. WHITEHEAD
The Stealing of America, 1983

Chocolate

It's not that chocolates are a substitute for love. Love is a substitute for chocolate. Chocolate is, let's face it, far more reliable than a man.

~ MIRANDA INGRAM

Chocolate causes certain endocrine glands to secrete hormones that affect your feelings and behavior by making you happy. Therefore, it counteracts depression, in turn reducing the stress of depression. Your stress-free life helps you maintain a youthful disposition, both physically and mentally. So, eat lots of chocolate!

~ ELAINE SHERMAN
Author of Book of Divine Indulgences

I never met a chocolate I didn't like.

~ DEANNA TROI
From the TV Series Star Trek: The Next Generation

Chocolate is cheaper than therapy and you don't need an appointment.

~ UNKNOWN

There are four basic food groups: milk chocolate, dark chocolate, white chocolate, and chocolate truffles.

~ UNKNOWN

All I really need is love, but a little chocolate now and then doesn't hurt!

~ LUCY VAN PELT (IN *PEANUTS* CARTOON)

Strength is the capacity to break a chocolate bar into four pieces with your bare hands—and then eat just one of the pieces.

~ JUDITH VIORST

Choice & Common Sense

When you make choices with you in mind, you have no regrets.

~ PATRICE BAKER
Speaker, www.PowerOfWords.com

The world is terrified by joyful women. Take a stand—be one anyway!

~ MARIANNE WILLIAMSON
Author of A Return to Love

Happiness for the average person may be said to flow largely from common sense—adapting one-self to circumstances—and a sense of humor.

~ BEATRICE LILLIE

Turn you mind off and look again. You will see it.

~ STEPHANIE MOLES
Founder of The Woman's Heart, www.TheWoman'sHeart.org

Every day we make choices, decisions about what and how our life will be. Each day we go forward or backwards in getting what we want in life. Sometimes we don't make the right choices, but we make the choice we thought best at the moment. We all make mistakes. It's learning from our mistakes and letting them go that determines our future.

~ DEBRA PESTRAK
Speaker, author, www.DebraPestrak.com

One's philosophy is not best expressed in words; it is expressed in the choices one makes. In the long run, we shape our lives and we shape ourselves. The process never ends until we die. And, the choices we make are ultimately our own responsibility.

~ ELEANOR ROOSEVELT

Falling in love consists merely in uncorking the imagination and bottling the common sense.

~ HELEN ROWLAND

Communication

We don't have to trample other people's feelings to express our own—speak your truth, speak from your heart for caring connections.

~ COLETTE CARLSON
Speaker, contributing author of Conversations on Success, www.colettecarlson.com

We often spend so much time taking care of the urgent; we miss addressing the important.

~ BETTY COLSTON

Your spontaneous heart-deep words often convey your true love with more grace and profundity than your rehearsed attempts to speak. This is so for all the patterns of your life.

~ DAVID DEIDA
Speaker, author of books on relationships, including It's A Guy Thing: An Owner's Manual For Women, *www.BlueTruth.org*

Look into my eyes and hear what I'm not saying, for my eyes speak louder than my voice ever will.

~ MARIELOU S. FLORENDO

We have to ask for what we want, or we won't get it. If we don't ask for what we want, we can't be surprised when we don't get it. We might ask for what we want and not get it, but if we don't ask, we almost certainly won't get it.

~ KATHELEN R. JOHNSON
www.TheTeachersVoice.com

Enthusiasm turns "I have to" into "I want to" and "I don't want to" into "I'm doing it anyway" and "It's not fun" into "I'll make this fun."

~ MARY MARCDANTE
Speaker, author, www.MaryMarcdante.com

Communication CONTINUED

Those who do not know how to weep with their whole heart don't know how to laugh either.
~ GOLDA MEIR

Until you say "No," you have said "Yes."
~ STEPHANIE MOLES
Founder of The Woman's Heart, www.TheWoman'sHeart.org

The most important words you will ever hear are the words you say to yourself.
~ MONA M. MOON
Speaker, www.MonaMoon.com

There's not enough appreciation in the world today. That's why I send a lot of thank you notes and handwritten messages. We all ought to be more kind to each other.
~ JULIA ROUSH

The most brilliant revelation I've had in understanding men was reading Deborah Tannen's book *Talking From 9 to 5,* which states that women nod our heads when we are in agreement; whereas men nod when they are listening—not necessarily agreeing! That explains *so* much!
~ SHERYL ROUSH
Speaker, author of Sparkle-Tudes! *and* Heart of A Mother, *www.SparklePresentations.com*

Improve your listening skills and watch your credibility increase.
~ JENNIFER ROUSSEAU SEDLOCK
www.JenniferSpeaks.com

Love is saying "I feel differently" instead of "You're wrong."
~ UNKNOWN

Count Your Blessings

If you woke up this morning with more health than illness . . . you are more blessed than the million who will not survive this week.

If you have never experienced the danger of battle, the loneliness of imprisonment, the agony of torture, or the pangs of starvation . . . you are ahead of 500 million people in the world.

If you can attend a church meeting without fear of harassment, arrest, torture, or death . . . you are more blessed than three billion people in the world.

If you have food in the refrigerator, clothes on your back, a roof overhead and a place to sleep . . . you are richer than 75% of this world.

If you have money in the bank, in your wallet, and spare change in a dish someplace . . . you are among the top 8% of the world's wealthy.

If your parents are still alive and still married . . . you are very rare, even in the United States.

If you hold up your head with a smile on your face and are truly thankful . . . you are blessed because the majority can, but most do not.

If you can hold someone's hand, hug them or even touch them on the shoulder . . . you are blessed because you can offer God's healing touch.

If you prayed yesterday and today . . . you are in the minority because you believe God does hear and answer prayers.

If you can read this message, you are more blessed than over two billion people in the world that cannot read at all.

Have a good day, count your blessings.

~ UNKNOWN

Courage

I'm not funny. What I am is brave.

~ LUCILLE BALL

Courage is fear that has said its prayers.

~ DOROTHY BERNARD

Waking up to the wonder of you, knowing that you are absolutely enough, embracing who you are fully and completely, relishing your life: that is fearless living.

~ RHONDA BRITTEN
Founder of the Fearless Living Institute, author of Fearless Loving: 8 Simple Truths That Will Change the Way You Date, Mate and Relate

Courage is like a muscle. We strengthen it with use.

~ RUTH GORDON

Having courage does not mean we feel no fear; it means acting despite fear in the most effective way we can.

~ MARSHA SINETAR

The only courage people need—is the courage to live their own dreams.

~ OPRAH WINFREY

. . . The true meaning of courage is to be afraid, and then, with your knees knocking and your heart racing, to step out of the way—even when that step makes sense to nobody but you.

~ OPRAH WINFREY

COURAGE, FAITH AND PERSISTENCE—
HOW I SURVIVED BREAST CANCER!

According to the American Cancer Society, one out of seven women will be diagnosed with Breast Cancer. It affects more of us than we can ever imagine. Since there had been no history in my maternal family line of breast cancer, I felt I was at a very small to no risk. Of course, it would never happen to me. On my father's side of the family, there were two sisters with breast cancer, one in her late forties and again in her seventies, and the other in her seventies when they were diagnosed.

Faithfully, I went for my yearly exams to my Ob/Gyn. Never had I had any lumps in my breasts during an exam. Although I was in my mid-forties, I had not yet had a mammogram. My list of reasons for not doing it and my excuses were probably just like yours if you haven't done it either. My doctor had advised upon getting one; but I didn't sense any urgency. I had just gone through pregnancy and nursing.

Considerably late in life, I gave birth to my son. I was busy being a new Mom, breastfeeding and basking in the glory of my little miracle. Fortunately, my pregnancy was fairly easy and I had a very healthy baby in spite of my age. Jason was 7 lbs., 8 oz. and 21" long! Big enough for me, thank you! My doctor advised that when I stopped breast-feeding to allow a little time and then we'd schedule a mammogram. Again, there was no urgency, just advice.

While I was nursing, the very tip of my nipple developed a very small sore.

I had had some difficulty nursing and some irritations; and this small sore seemed no more than part of that. When I first pointed it out to my doctor, she said it was nothing. She thought it was a breast-feeding irritation.

Courage CONTINUED

Several more months went by. I stopped breast-feeding and gave my nipple time to heal. It didn't. Conscious that my body didn't usually take this long to heal, I went in to see another doctor and get a second opinion. She said it's either nothing at all or a very rare form of breast cancer; she scheduled a mammogram. Immediately following the mammogram was my appointment with the surgeon and he diagnosed me with a rare breast cancer called Paget's Disease. The dismay and shock I felt made it so hard for me to even find my way out of the doctor's office! As I sat in my car in the hospital parking garage, I screamed and screamed, wondering if I would live long enough to raise my now two-year-old son.

After the initial shock, there were moments when I would feel a tremendous calm in spite of all the emotional chaos. When I could be in touch with my feelings, I knew that God was with me through this entire ordeal. Two weeks after diagnosis, and just two weeks before Christmas, I had a mastectomy!

On Christmas Eve, my gift was the removal of the drainage tubes from surgery. I went through chemotherapy treatment and lost 95% of my hair. Although I never went completely bald, wigs and hats became my new fashion statement. I loved that I could put my head out of the car window and not mess up my hair!

Every woman's experience with cancer is very personal and no two people seem to have the exact same experience even though we all go through similar treatments. One thing that was amazing to me, people that you barely know will step up and lend their help and support in unexpected and amazing ways. And sometimes, people whom you would expect to be supportive are not. Many close friends and family are at a total loss as what to do to help a loved one. They are so afraid for you and for themselves.

Courage CONTINUED

It was a conscious decision on my part to ask as many people as possible to add me to their prayers. Although I am a spiritual woman, I would not say I am deeply religious. This was not a time to be shy, coy or modest. My life was at risk! Many women and men who didn't know me or vice versa, included me in their prayers and on prayer boards. I firmly believe their prayers made a huge difference in my getting through the cancer as well as I did. Some people even today keep me in their prayers even though the obvious cancer is gone; and I have been cancer free for nearly three years now. I welcome and appreciate those prayers and always say thank you. The power of prayer is strong.

An example of my getting through fairly well are, my red blood cell count levels never went below normal even though I had months of chemotherapy. Some people loose their blood count levels after the first treatment. I had my chemotherapies on Fridays. One Friday, I was to join my friends on an annual trip to the mountains in Idyllwild for hiking and relaxing. On Saturday, the day of the hike, I decided to go and just go for as far as I could or was comfortable for me. As the trail wound up the mountain, I found the view and the fresh air exhilarating and energizing. I ended up hiking that day for about five to seven miles! Now that may not sound like a lot when you're healthy; but after chemo, it's quite a feat. Needless to say the next day I was very tired; but it was a good kind of tired; and I felt proud of myself for even being able to do it.

I came to realize that although having cancer is an awful experience, God meant for me to go through it for some reason. It is also not the worst challenge a person can have. I can look at the challenges that others go through and feel I am blessed that mine was "only" breast cancer. There is always something worse. The attitude you chose to have in a crisis is also of major importance to the success of the outcome. No, it's not easy. But find what is important to you and focus on that. For me, it was living to raise my son for a long, long time to come. We may not understand what God wants from us, but we can have trust and just go with it as best we can.

Have you heard, the concept "make lemonade out of the lemons?" For most of us, unless we are challenged to do this, it is only a saying. It is real. No matter what you go through and the challenges you face, there are sweet spots. Don't get me wrong; it doesn't take the tragedy out of things. But when we look for even the smallest, tiniest glimmer of what is positive out of the experience you can and will have a new perspective. When I asked my Aunt Mary, who had gone through breast cancer two times, with two mastectomies years apart, "How did this experience change you?" What she shared with me is what I have since heard many other women say in similar ways, "You quit sweating the small stuff. I learned to appreciate my children even more. Every day is precious." Like Aunt Mary, I smile now when my son does something that might have made me angry before. Now, I tend to think, it's not that important and things happen. In the grand scheme of things, it doesn't really matter. I am thankful to be here for him and he for me, because he is the most precious thing in the world to me.

Did you as a child ever envy the guys because they could take their shirts off on a hot summer day? Well, I did. Girls didn't get to do that. After the mastectomy, in my rare case of sick-sense-of-humor, I wondered, "If I had had a double mastectomy would that mean I could take my shirt off in the summer and no one would care?" Obviously, I came to the conclusion that, "Yes, many would care," but it was a rather funny thought just the same!

More and more women can—and do survive breast cancer. If you find anything unusual for your own body and how it would normally

Courage

react, get it checked! See your doctor. You are your best super sleuth when it comes to your own body and health. Don't ignore those little things that just don't seem quite right. Early diagnosis is best. The women I know that have lost their lives to breast cancer often ignored their early warning signs. I was on Tamoxifen for two years and am now on Aromasin for an expected 3 more years. More people need to be aware that breast cancer is not just about lumps and not just about women. Men can have breast cancer, too.

Help get the word out. Emails are circulating in an attempt to inform people. It seems to be more prevalent than initially thought. Today, I volunteer for the American Cancer Society, and donate a percentage of my sales to the ACS.

If you know of someone going through breast cancer and are wondering what you might be able to do to help them, go to www.ElnAlbert.com, a free article, "How To Help Her With Cancer," with dozens of little ideas on how you can help a loved one. All those little things make a big difference. Throughout my ordeal, I choose to have courage, faith and persistence. I trust if you should find yourself in a similar situation, you will find the strength to do the same.

~ ELN ALBERT
Speaker, author of The Magic of Moms, *addressing the unique motherly qualities working women bring to the workplace. Participate in the research survey by going to www.ElnAlbert.com.*

LESSON IN COURAGE—
JO ANN'S STORY

*T*he first time I ever jumped out of a plane, I was with my friend Jo Ann. We went together to a drop zone at Perris, California, to watch a fundraiser called "Jump for the Cause." Nearly two hundred women would attempt a record-setting formation to raise money for Breast Cancer research. We went to this event because Jo

Courage CONTINUED

Ann had been diagnosed again with cancer. This time, the cancer was more aggressive and harder to beat, and she needed some inspiration to get her through the months ahead.

Jo Ann and I watched the formation build high in the sky. When we saw it, all these women in pink jumpsuits were just a tiny pinpoint, just barely visible. It was so exciting that we decided we would participate in the fundraiser by doing tandem skydives.

In a tandem skydive, you go out of the plane strapped to an instructor who has the parachute, the training, and the knowledge. The instructor does everything—provides stability during freefall, negotiates the landing, and pulls the ripcord, and while the tandem student is just along for the ride.

That tandem jump was my first skydive, but not Jo Ann's. She had done her first tandem jump when she received her second cancer diagnosis twelve years before. When she received that diagnosis, she knew from experience what would lay ahead—the chemotherapy, radiation treatments, surgery, physical and emotional scarring. She knew she had to do something to build her courage and prepare her for the coming trial. So she did a tandem skydive.

There's nothing like jumping out of a plane for building your courage! You know that despite the safety precautions, the instructor's expertise and experience, you could be seriously injured or even killed. You look down at the ground from 12,000 feet. You look death right in the face, and jump anyway. The experience proves you have courage, that you can do things even though you are very afraid.

So Jo Ann and I signed up that day for our tandem jumps. We received a short lesson on what to expect, then got on the plane with our instructors. The 20-minute plane ride to jump altitude gave me plenty of time to reconsider this foolhardy decision and to imagine all the things that I was certain would go wrong.

Courage <small>CONTINUED</small>

I was so scared in that plane that I could hardly speak. I was scared of falling, of dying, of losing control. I didn't know until later that Jo Ann faced a different level of fear. You see, the cancer had spread to her lungs, and she didn't think she would be able to breathe in the thinner air at 12,000 feet. But we each made it to the door of the plane with our instructors, and we each jumped out the door despite our fears. The experience was truly overwhelming. After my instructor opened the canopy and we drifted gracefully toward the ground, I was weeping, for my friend and for the loss I knew was coming, and for the beauty of the earth from 12,000 feet. And when we landed, my legs were so rubbery I could not stand up. But I did it; I had jumped out of a plane. And it was Jo Ann's courage that got me there.

Three months later, Jo Ann finally succumbed to the cancer she had struggled against for nearly twenty years. It was her courage and her refusal to give in that gave her—and our friendship—so much time.

Courage isn't the absence of fear. Courage is acting despite your fear, acting even though you are deathly afraid. Jo Ann looked death squarely in the face—in her two skydives and throughout her four bouts with cancer—and she acted anyway.

I owe so much to Jo Ann. She taught me about courage, about being brave enough to do what you've got to do. Her example got me through an abusive marriage and a painful divorce. Her courage taught me to stand up for myself at work and within my family. And it was her courage that helped me begin a student program to earn my skydiving license. Now I build my courage every time I jump, and I wave hello to Jo Ann, who I know is watching me and smiling. Thank you, Jo Ann.

~ MARGARET CONNERY
Speaker and trainer

Dance

There are short-cuts to happiness, and dancing is one of them.
~ VICKI BAUM

I always thought that if I learned to stand on my own two feet I could dance through life. It's true.
~ NATALIE D. BRECHER, CPM®
Speaker, author of Business without Biceps: The Untold Truths of Women in Business and How to Make Them Work for You

Dancing is like dreaming with your feet!
~ CONSTANZE

The truest expression of a people is in its dance and in its music. Bodies never lie.
~ AGNES DE MILLE

To dance is to be out of yourself. Larger, more beautiful, more powerful.
~ AGNES DE MILLE

Dancing is the poetry of the foot.
~ JOHN DRYDEN

Dancers are the athletes of God.
~ ALBERT EINSTEIN

Everybody can dance. Our feet will follow our heart much better than the head!
~ TERRY FREEMAN
Aerobic, Dance, Pilates, and Yoga instructor

Dance CONTINUED

The dance is a poem of which each movement is a word.
~ MATA HARI

To watch us dance is to hear our hearts speak.
~ HOPI INDIAN SAYING

Dance is the hidden language of the soul. . . . Movement never lies. It is a barometer telling the state of the soul's weather.
~ MARTHA GRAHAM
American dancer, choreographer

Dancing is wonderful training for girls, it's the first way you learn to guess what a man is going to do before he does it.
~ CHRISTOPHER MORLEY

I see dance being used as communication between body and soul, to express what it too deep to find for words.
~ RUTH ST. DENIS

Only the wise can dance the rhythm of life.
~ UNKNOWN

You can dance anywhere, even if only in your heart.
~ UNKNOWN

Dancing is the perpendicular expression of a horizontal desire.
~ UNKNOWN

Socrates learned to dance when he was seventy because he felt that an essential part of himself had been neglected.
~ UNKNOWN

Dating

Dating is where you practice being yourself.
~ RHONDA BRITTEN
Speaker, author of Fearless Living

Your looks may grab my eye, but your personality will hold my heart.
~ DEBRA HALE

Wait for the boy who pursues you, the one who will make an ordinary moment seem magical, the kind of boy who brings out the best in you and makes you want to be a better person.
　　Wait for the boy who will be your best friend.
　　Wait for the boy who makes you smile like no other boy makes you smile and when he smiles you know he needs you.
　　Wait for the boy who wants to show you off the the world when you are in sweats and have no makeup on, but appreciates it when you get all dolled up for him.
　　And most of all wait for the boy who will put you at the center of his universe, because obviously he's at the center of yours.
~ MANDI NOWLIN, AGE 21
Daughter and sister

I find the dating ritual archaic. I firmly believe in like, lust and love at first sight. When I experience all three with one person, they will declare a national holiday!
~ BECKY PALMER, AGE 52, NEVER MARRIED

Never think that you are not good enough for anyone;
always ask yourself if they are good enough for you.
~ UNKNOWN

Dating CONTINUED

THE MAKING OF A BEAUTY QUEEN

*T*he discovery of the truth that "beauty is in the eye of the beholder" has never been so profound for me as when my naturally trim friend reframed my view of my full figure. As was my habit, I was criticizing myself out loud to her for not having lost weight. My verbal assault about my body was an attempt to redeem myself for my defect. I'd always felt that if I could put myself down before others could, I'd look better in their eyes. Boy was I surprised when she cast a new light on my downbeat view of myself.

"Men aren't attracted to me because I'm overweight," I said.
"Really! I would think the opposite. Your body is so soft and cuddly. I'd think a man would love to wrap his arms around you."
"Hmmm!" I listened intently.
"Look at me." she continued. "I'm so skinny that my hip bones stick out. I'm always afraid that they jab at my boyfriend when we hug."

Struck with enlightenment, my fresh attitude opened the door to a new world of dating, Previously, if a man showed interest in me, I'd reject him because I'd think there was something wrong with him. My philosophy was that of Woody Allen who said, "I'd never become part of club that would have me a member." Now armed with new self-acceptance, enter . . . Jonathan.

The glow in his eyes when he'd take me in his arms was like a wave of Cinderella's fairy godmother's wand. I was transformed. The years of candle-lit rooms and many nights of a red rose-covered bed, held even more magic for me. It melted my body down to a size and a half smaller.

~ NIKKI GOLDMAN
Speaker, author of Success for the Diet Dropout: Proven Strategies for Women Who Want to Stop Hating their Bodies, *www.DrNikkiGoldman.com*

Daughters

LESSONS LEARNED FROM MY DAUGHTER

- *Not all birds die when rescued and put in a box.*
- *Laundry can be done every two weeks if one has enough underwear.*
- *Books are to be read in the bathtub.*
- *Why do today what can be put off until midnight.*
- *Not all shy children stay that way.*
- *There is strength in being tall and beautiful.*
- *Food should be fast and tasty.*
- *Why drink water when one can slurp an icee.*
- *Small children and little sisters are extremely annoying.*
- *Large garden caterpillars are actually tomorrow's butterflies.*
- *There's no such thing as having too many stuffed animals.*
- *Closets should be properly organized using color-coded hangers.*
- *Some children become athletic in high school.*
- *There is strength in being quiet and gentle.*
- *Anyone can be suspect in stealing a chicken.*
- *Only your little sister can be suspect when something is missing around the house.*
- *Respect can be earned without being loud and pushy.*
- *One can never read too many books.*
- *Bed sheets need never be changed; they always work the way they are.*
- *Vacuuming is optional as well.*
- *Forget cleaning sinks and toilets while we're at it.*
- *Spare time should be spent reading, not cleaning.*
- *Some children are admired by many people for helping and doing wonderful things that you'll never know about.*
- *There's no such thing as overfeeding a chicken.*
- *One can never see too many movies, too many cats, too much clothing.*
- *One can love a chicken.*

~ MARY GAY ROUSH, RN
Mother of two daughters, "Things I've Learned from Serina"

MY IRIS GAYLE

My Iris Gale is quite a girl
For her each night I knit and purl,
And sit and wonder with furrowed brow,
If it is possible, and why and how.

Her little form stirs in my heart,
A love that words cannot impart.
The thought of her makes my heart leap.
I can't believe she's mine to keep.

She has a pert little turned up nose,
With a darling mouth like a pink tea rose.
And when she smiles her face lights up
Like the morning sun on a buttercup.

Then when into her room I creep,
To watch as she smiles in her sleep,
I know that nothing can replace
The love I feel for my angel face.

Yes, Iris Gayle is quite a girl
For her each night I knit and purl,
And sit and wonder with furrowed brow,
If it is possible, and why and how.

~ ROSALIE FERRER KRAMER
Speaker, poet, author of Dancing in the Dark: Things My Mother Never Told Me
www.authorsden.com/rosaliefkramer

Daughters CONTINUED

There's something like a line of gold thread running through a man's words when he talks to his daughter, and gradually over the years it gets to be long enough for you to pick up in your hands and weave into a cloth that feels like love itself.

~ JOHN GREGORY BROWN
Decorations in a Ruined Cemetery, *1994*

We have every reason to look forward into the future with hope and excitement. Fear nothing and no one. Work honestly. Be good, be happy. And remember that each of you is unique, your soul your own, irreplaceable, and individual in the miracle of your mortal frame.

~ PEARL S. BUCK

ACTING LIKE BOYS?

*S*itting on the park's cold cement with my feet in warm sand is when I first had this awareness. Truth be told, I was eavesdropping on a Mother's Playgroup as I helped my own two daughters build a castle nearby. "Heather doesn't like dolls . . . she prefers to build with her brother's Lego." The statement itself, didn't throw me. It was the tone and air of superiority in the Mother's voice that did. When did it become "better" for little girls to act more like boys?

My husband and I have every intention in the world of raising our daughters to have a powerful voice. I want them to get in the game and be comfortable taking risks instead of watching from the sidelines, and we provide healthy feedback and activities accordingly. Yet, we're also proud of their ability to be nurturing and loving and tell them so when appropriate.

Maybe that Mother's comment wouldn't burn so deeply if I didn't feel that it was just another way that women pay lip service to celebrating our strengths. We can help our daughters by giving them

Daughters

permission to be clear, direct and assertive even if it doesn't appear "ladylike." We can help our daughters by praising them for their skills and abilities instead of just their beauty. We can help our daughters by being proud of our own bodies just the way they are. Until mothers can model those behaviors, their daughters will pay a price. Perhaps that's all the mother in the park was trying to say.

~ COLETTE CARLSON, MA
Speaker, contributing author of Conversations on Success, *www.colettecarlson.com*

A son is a son till he takes him a wife, a daughter is a daughter all of her life.

~ IRISH SAYING

A daughter is a mother's gender partner, her closest ally in the family confederacy, an extension of her self. And mothers are their daughters' role model, their biological and emotional road map, the arbiter of all their relationships.

~ VICTORIA SECUNDA

I always had three rules when raising my daughter . . . to know her friends well, to choose battles wisely, and to treat her with respect.

~ DEBRA SIMPSON
www.DebraSimpson.com

The little girl dances to the song of love in the grown ups heart.

~ CATHERINE TILLEY
Founder of the Institute for Global Healing and Publisher of WISE Publications
www.theglobalvoice.com

Daughters CONTINUED

ADOPTED DAUGHTERS AND
THEIR CIRCLE OF LOVE

*I*f I ever felt an expression of love from my daughters, this was one beautiful experience that will forever stay with me . . . Last Tuesday, my birthday, my daughters asked me to take them to an activity in the evening. When I arrived to pick them up, they emerged from the house carrying a cake adorned with at least a dozen lighted candles. Their faces were aglow from the candlelight, left an indelible imprint on my mind, as they sang "Happy Birthday." In their scurry to get the cake ready on time, the cool icing caused the freshly baked cake still warm out of the oven to fall apart on one side. For me this birthday cake was made with so much love, I never would have noticed. It was perfect. A memory to savor forever. To top it off, they secretly planned a little surprise party at my favorite pizza restaurant! My daughter Lauren visited with her birthmother just before Christmas. The birthmother and I have been in contact via telephone and email and this reconnection has been unbelievable in a circle of love.

~ CONNIE HOPE DIAMOND
Beaming mother of two adopted daughters

Death & Grieving

BEYOND THE SKY
Much like the sun and moon or tide
Memories can never die.
Those we love dwell forever there
In distant mists and evening air.
That is where your loved ones wait
Beyond the clouds, pleasant state
So do not grieve that they've gone there
To a place of the seasons always fair.
Heal knowing you can join them someday.
Do not let grief stand in your way,
Since if your loved one's in your heart,
You'll never really have to part.
For in a place just 'round the bend,
You will surely meet again,
Where in the fog and evening air,
All our loved ones will be there.

And we will all meet again.

~ ROSALIE FERRER KRAMER
Speaker, poet, author, www.authorsden.com/rosaliefkramer

Poets have said that the reason to have children is to give yourself immortality. Immortality? Now that I have five children, my only hope is that they are all out of the house before I die.

~ BILL COSBY

When you are sorrowful look again in your heart, and you shall see that in truth you are weeping for that which has been your delight.

~ KAHLIL GIBRAN

Death & Grieving CONTINUED

The death of someone we know always reminds us that we are still alive—perhaps for some purpose which we ought to re-examine.
~ MIGNON MCLAUGHLIN

The idea is to die young as late as possible.
~ ASHLEY MONTAGU

We understand death for the first time when he puts his hand upon one whom we love.
~ MADAME DE STAEL

God made death so we'd know when to stop.
~ STEVEN STILES

There are things that we don't want to happen but have to accept, things we don't want to know but have to learn, and people we can't live without but have to let go.
~ UNKNOWN

Whenever someone you know dies, or makes their transition, I believe you now have angels that you know.
~ OPRAH WINFREY

Memory is a way of holding onto the things you love, the things you are, the things you never want to lose.
~ FROM THE TV SERIES *THE WONDER YEARS*

LOVING ARMS
A song written for Karl's Mom before she died in 1993

Please if you must go, then let me know . . .
where will I feel your loving arms
Is it too much to want for the touch . . .
I have been used to all my life
I am afraid, a decision is made . . .
but I am less than willing
So if you must go, then let me know . . .
where will I feel your loving arms

Please could you disguise or look through the eyes . . .
used by a perfect stranger
Then, whether or not, this lesson is taught . . .
I will be in your loving arms
In all that I do, I'm thinking of you . . .
and it will bless my life
So please, if you must go, then let me know . . .
please let me feel your loving arms

I am afraid a decision is made . . .
and I am less than willing . . . so
If you must go, then let me know . . .
where will I feel your loving arms
If you must go, then let me know . . .
please let me feel your. . . . loving arm
Here is where I will feel your . . . loving arms

~ KARL ANTHONY
Singer, author of Songwriter
www.KarlAnthony.com

Death & Grieving

WHEN YOUR MOTHER PASSES

You hold her hand impossibly tight,
Listening, listening, with all of your might,
You want to hear, just once more for you,
"I love you, and I'm proud of all that you do."

Instead, she struggles for each last breath,
Her eyes closed tight—her body near death.
You want to hold her, but you're afraid she'll break,
How can she leave you? So much of you she'll take.

You wait for a signal—some kind of sign,
That she'll be all right for the rest of time.
You know she needs approval from you,
That it's all right to go away from view.

Her breath grows more labored,
You wonder what to do.
Who will tell you, "I'm so proud of you."
Who will remember from day one?
Where will your memories go, when her life is done?

The hour is near, she's grown so tired.
She did her job—she served her time.
She needs to know it's her last day.
She needs to know that you'll be okay.

It's so hard, you take a break.
The day is still, your body does ache.
You sit down next to the open door,
The curtains blow—you're alone no more.

The angels have come to take her away.
"I know you're here, talk to me," you say.
Her breathing changes—soft as a baby.
Is it Daddy or Grandma she sees? Well, maybe.

You grab her hand and know it's time.
The words must come—the words sublime.
I'll be okay, Mom, it's okay to go,
You'll always be with me—I love you so.

It's okay to go,
You'll always be with me—I love you so.
Within seconds your dear mother breathes no more,
Her body is there, but her spirit does soar.
Her soul has moved on and you're all alone,
"Mom is gone," you cry, "now she'll never phone."

You do the right thing to see her off to eternity,
The proper casket, ceremony and serendipity.
Your body's empty, you have no heart,
Your mother's gone—She bore your start.

Death & Grieving

How can you live without the womb,
That was your first and most loving room?
Where is the meaning when Mom is dead?
Who will you try to make happy instead?

Days and months pass by like sand,
You cry and cry and search the land.
Who will love you unconditionally?
"No one," you say, "Its up to me."

Now you can do it because Mom's moved in,
She lives in your heart where she's Mother Hen.
You'll never be lonely—you're living for two,
Moms never leave, they just become you.

~ JUDITH PARKER HARRIS, SPEAKER
Author of Master Challenges in Your Life and Move From Blocked to Block-Buster
www.blockedtoblock-buster.com, www.culturalblockbusters.com

I Wrote

When they said my sons would die,
I did not rant, I did not cry,
I wrote.

If there was no one to tell,
I did not moan, I did not yell,
I just wrote.

Times I thought I could not cope,
I grasped my pen, I gathered hope,
And I wrote some more.

I cannot explain it now,
But it healed my soul somehow,
When I wrote.

And I know it's been worthwhile.
Since poetry brought back my smile.
As I wrote.

Now I'm writing more and more,
I cannot stop, I can't keep score.
I just write.

And I must keep on writing; it's the reason I'm still sane.

~ ROSALIE FERRER KRAMER
Speaker, poet, author of Dancing in the Dark: Things My Mother Never Told Me
www.authorsden.com/rosaliefkramer

Death & Grieving CONTINUED

I know for certain that we never lose the people we love, even to death. They continue to participate in every act, thought and decision we make. Their love leaves an indelible imprint in our memories. We find comfort in knowing that our lives have been enriched by having shared their love.

~ LEO BUSCAGLIA

Loss is a byproduct of living.

~ KIRSTI A. DYER, MD, MS

The path to healing from a loss is different for each person, one which may have many unexpected twists and turns, but a road that has been traveled by many. Grief is a powerful, universal feeling, but it is survivable.

~ KIRSTI A. DYER, MD, MS

To live is to suffer, to survive is to find some meaning in the suffering.

~ ROBERTA FLACK

Grief is a journey, often perilous and without clear direction, that must be taken. The experience of grieving cannot be ordered or categorized, hurried or controlled, pushed aside or ignored indefinitely. It is inevitable as breathing, as change, as love. It may be postponed, but it will not be denied.

~ MOLLY FUMIA

Grief is the most patient and persistent of all of life's companions. It is an ancient, universal power that links all human beings together.

~ MOLLY FUMIA
Safe Passage

Deep sobs—
That start beneath my heart
and hold my body in a grip that hurts.
The lump that swells inside my throat
brings pain that tries to choke.
Then tears course down my cheeks—
I drop my head in my so empty hands
abandoning myself to deep dark grief
and know that with the passing time
will come relief.
That though the pain may stay
There soon will come a day
When I can say her name
and be at peace.

~ NORAH LENEY

Suffering is not an elective, it is a core course in the University of Life.

~ STEVEN J. LAWSON

You need to face the pain and the fear and walk through the Grief.

~ DR. PHIL MCGRAW

\Great joys make us love the world. Great sadnesses make us understand the world.

~ KENT NERBURN

We are healed of a suffering only by experiencing it in full.

~ MARCEL PROUST

Death & Grieving <small>CONTINUED</small>

FEELING GRIEF

Grief is a tidal wave that over takes you,
smashes down upon you with unimaginable force,
sweeps you up into its darkness,
where you tumble and crash against unidentifiable surfaces,
only to be thrown out on an unknown beach,
bruised, reshaped . . .
It is the ashes from which the phoenix rises,
and the mettle of rebirth.

It returns life to the living dead.
It teaches that there is nothing absolutely true or untrue . . .

Grief will make a new person out of you,
if it doesn't kill you in the making.

~ STEPHANIE ERICSSON

People in mourning have to come to grips with death before they can live again. Mourning can go on for years and years. It doesn't end after a year, that's a false fantasy. It usually ends when people realize that they can live again, that they can concentrate their energies on their lives as a whole, and not on their hurt, and guilt and pain.

~ ELISABETH KÜBLER-ROSS

An ungrieved loss remains forever alive in our unconscious, which has no sense of time.

~ B.G. SIMOS

Do It Anyway

People are often unreasonable, illogical, and self-centered;
Forgive them anyway.

If you are kind, people may accuse you of selfish, ulterior motives;

Be kind anyway.

If you are successful you will win some false friends

and true enemies;

Succeed anyway.

If you are honest and frank, people may cheat you;

Be honest and frank anyway.

What you spend years building, someone could destroy overnight;

Build anyway.

If you find serenity and happiness, they may be jealous;

Be happy anyway.

The good you do today, people will often forget tomorrow;

Do good anyway.

Give the world the best you have, and it may never be enough;

Give the world the best you've got anyway.

You see, in the final analysis, it is between you and God;
It was never between you and them anyway.

~ MOTHER TERESA

Dogs

It is possible to buy love, you can buy a dog!

~ MONICA DENNY
Mother of twin teenage boys

You enter into a certain amount of madness when you marry a person with pets.

~ NORA EPHRON

Women and cats will do as they please and men and dogs should relax and get used to the idea.

~ ROBERT A. HEINLEIN

Don't accept your dog's admiration as conclusive evidence that you are wonderful.

~ ANN LANDERS

No animal should ever jump up on the dining-room furniture unless absolutely certain that he can hold his own in the conversation.

~ FRAN LEBOWITZ

Did you ever walk into a room and forget why you walked in? I think that is how dogs spend their lives.

~ SUE MURPHY

Pets have a way of knowing what's going on with you, how you are feeling. There is nothing like giving your pet a big hug and taking advantage of that unconditional love.

~ DEBRA PESTRAK
Speaker, author, www.DebraPestrak.com

Dogs CONTINUED

The greatest love is a mother's; then a dog's; then a sweetheart's.
~ POLISH PROVERB

I think dogs are the most amazing creatures; they give unconditional love. For me they are the role model for being alive.
~ GILDA RADNER

From the dog's point of view, his master is an elongated and abnormally cunning dog.
~ MABEL LOUISE ROBINSON

My husband and I are either going to buy a dog or have a child. We can't decide whether to ruin our carpets or ruin our lives.
~ RITA RUDNER

Ever consider what they must think of us? I mean, here we come back from a grocery store with the most amazing haul—chicken, pork, half cow. They just think we're the greatest hunters on earth!
~ ANNE TYLER

One reason a dog can be such a comfort when you're feeling blue is that he doesn't try to find out why.
~ UNKNOWN

My goal in life is to be as good of a person my dog already thinks I am.
~ UNKNOWN

My little dog—a heartbeat at my feet.
~ EDITH WHARTON

Dreams

Every obstacle we encounter is a natural and necessary step on the road to achieving our dreams.

~ CYNTHIA KERSEY
Speaker, author of Unstoppable, *www.unstoppable.net*

Do your dream now! You'll find that once you commit to yourself, the Universe gives you unlimited support, and creates even more options for you. YOU CAN DO IT!

~ CATHERINE ANN NARY, AKA "CAN-DO"

Dreams draw us forward, towards an even more fulfilling, joyful and abundant life. Dreams build bridges between where we are now and where we can be in the future whether that means tomorrow, six months from now or ten years from now. Fueling our inner drive, they make our feet light, our tasks exciting instead of burdensome and our hopes infinitely possible.

~ JULIE JORDAN SCOTT, WWW.5PASSIONS.COM

Advance confidently in the direction of your dream and dare to BE the heroine in your own story.

~ MARILYN SPRAGUE-SMITH, M.ED.
Co-Author of The Princess Principle: Women Helping Women Discover Their Royal Spirit, *www.ThePrincessPrinciple.com*

What if we're all meant to be what we secretly dream?
What would you ask if you knew you could have anything?
Like the mighty oak sleeps in the heart of a seed . . .
Are there miracles in you and me?
What would I do today . . . If I Were Brave?

~ JANA STANFIELD
Singer, songwriter, from the song If I Were Brave, *www.JanaStanfield.com*

Estrogen

10 Ways to Know if You Have "Estrogen Issues"

1. Everyone around you has an attitude problem.
2. You're adding chocolate chips to your cheese omelet.
3. The dryer has shrunk every last pair of your jeans.
4. Your husband is suddenly agreeing to everything you say.
5. You're using your cellular phone to dial up every bumper sticker that says: "How's my driving? Call 1-800-"
6. Everyone's head looks like an invitation to batting practice.
7. Everyone seems to have just landed here from "outer space."
8. You can't believe they don't make a tampon bigger than Super Plus.
9. You're sure that everyone is scheming to drive you crazy.
10. The ibuprofen bottle is empty and you bought it yesterday.

~Anonymous

◆ ◆ ◆

I'm out of estrogen and I have a gun.
~ BUMPER STICKER

Next Mood Swing: 6 Minutes
~ BUMPER STICKER

Don't think of it as getting hot flashes. Think of it as your inner child playing with matches.
~ UNKNOWN

Faith

Faith is like radar that sees through the fog.

~ CORRIE TEN BOOM
Tramp for the Lord

Faith is putting all your eggs in God's basket, then counting your blessings before they hatch.

~ RAMONA C. CARROLL

Lift your sights. Look at the stars, especially when things seem darkest. Know that there is a higher power in the universe. You are not alone.

~ JO CONDRILL
Speaker, author of Take Charge of Your Life: Dare to Pursue Your Dreams, *www.goalminds.com*

It's the moment you think you can't that you realize you can.

~ CELINE DION

Faith really does affect the very core of who we are!
Our perception of God will determine the lives we live.

~ PSALMS 115: 2-8, PSALMS 135: 15-18

Having faith in a Source greater than—and one with—myself has empowered me to breakthrough every setback in my life—and I would not trade any of those events for the character it's developed in me. God is always working in my life! I choose every moment to walk with faith!

~ SHERYL ROUSH
Speaker, author of Sparkle-Tudes! *and* Heart of A Mother, *www.SparklePresentations.com*

A little faith will bring your soul to heaven,
but a lot of faith will bring heaven to your soul.

~ UNKNOWN

Falling in Love

When I look into your eyes, I see the light of a new day
Then my fears begin to melt away
We begin to cross the line between love and hate
And take steps to control our fate
For there is no better way to say
You are important to me in every way.

~ PATRICE C. BAKER
Speaker, life coach, author of The Power of Words: Poetry and Prose for Powerful Living,
www.ThePowerOfWords.com

You were standing there, holding out your heart for all to see, and in that instant, I knew I loved you.

~ FROM THE TV SERIES *BUFFY, THE VAMPIRE SLAYER*

Mumps, measles, and puppy love are terrible after twenty.

~ MIGNON MCLAUGHLIN

No one can understand love who has not experienced infatuation. And no one can understand infatuation, no matter how many times he has experienced it.

~ MIGNON MCLAUGHLIN

Falling in love and fixing a broken heart have something in common: they both take time.

~ SHENEA SHELFER

To fall in love is easy, even to remain in it is not difficult; our human loneliness is cause enough. But it is a hard quest worth making to find a comrade through whose steady presence one becomes steadily the person one desires to be.

~ ANNA LOUISE STRONG
Journalist, author

Falling in Love CONTINUED

I'll never forget the day I first realized that he liked me more than just a friend. One early morning he called me up and told me that he just had to bring me my mail today. I said that it wasn't necessary because I really wasn't expecting anything important. But when he made it sound so important that he bring my mail today, I said okay. So, just about an hour later, for it was quite a distance he had to travel, he arrived at my door looking great and wearing a great big smile. We talked a few minutes and then when I asked him for my mail, he looked around, laughed, blushed a little and said, "Oh no! I forgot it!" We both laughed and nothing more was said about it, but inside, I was smiling and dancing around because just then, I knew, that he liked me more than just a friend!

~ CATHERINE TILLEY
Founder of the Institute for Global Healing and Publisher of WISE Publications
www.theglobalvoice.com

You will never forget your first love. That's what makes it so special. You love so hard, so deeply, and so intensely because you don't know any different. It's the best until it is over. Then you hurt like you've never been hurt before. Eventually you love again, but you love differently. You will love more carefully, more cautiously. Just know that there is so much more love waiting for you, but there will only be one first.

~ UNKNOWN

Infatuation is when you think he's as sexy as Robert Redford, as smart as Henry Kissinger, as noble as Ralph Nader, as funny as Woody Allen, and as athletic as Jimmy Conners. Love is when you realize that he's as sexy as Woody Allen, as smart as Jimmy Connors, as funny as Ralph Nader, as athletic as Henry Kissinger and nothing like Robert Redford—but you'll take him anyway.

~ JUDITH VIORST, *REDBOOK*, 1975

Family

A Housewife's Lament

I've washed many pairs of dirty hands.
And cleaned a zillion pots and pans.
I've removed spots from the new beige carpet,
And made endless trips to the super market
I have tripped countless times on a toy in the hall,
And scrubbed the marks from the ivory wall.
Now I'm ready to run or to fly,
To the land where pants are always dry
Where husbands don't come home and say,
"What, darling, did you do today?"

~ ROSALIE FERRER KRAMER
Speaker, poet, author of Dancing in the Dark: Things My Mother Never Told Me
www.authorsden.com/rosaliefkramer

To us, family means putting your arms around each other and being there.

~ BARBARA BUSH

The family. We were a strange little band of characters trudging through life sharing diseases and toothpaste, coveting one another's desserts, hiding shampoo, borrowing money, locking each other out of our rooms, inflicting pain and kissing to heal it in the same instant, loving, laughing, defending, and trying to figure out the common thread that bound us all together.

~ ERMA BOMBECK

Other things may change us, but we start and end with the family.

~ ANTHONY BRANDT

Family CONTINUED

When you look at your life, the greatest happinesses are family happinesses.
~ DR. JOYCE BROTHERS

Are we not like two volumes of one book?
~ MARCELINE DESBORDES-VALMORE

Family: A social unit where the father is concerned with parking space, the children with outer space, and the mother with closet space.
~ EVAN ESAR

If you ever start feeling like you have the goofiest, craziest, most dysfunctional family in the world, all you have to do is go to a state fair. Because five minutes at the fair, you'll be going, "you know, we're alright. We are dang near royalty."
~ JEFF FOXWORTHY

The great gift of family life is to be intimately acquainted with people you might never even introduce yourself to, had life not done it for you.
~ KENDALL HAILEY
Author of The Day I Became an Autodidact

Where we love is home, home that our feet may leave, but not our hearts.
~ OLIVER WENDELL HOLMES
Physician, poet, humorist

Call it a clan, call it a network, call it a tribe, call it a family. Whatever you call it, whoever you are, you need one.
~ JANE HOWARD-FELDMAN

Family CONTINUED

The informality of family life is a blessed condition that allows us to become our best while looking our worst.

~ MARGE KENNEDY

In some families, please is described as the magic word. In our house, however, it was sorry.

~ MARGARET LAURENCE

Family is just accident. . . . They don't mean to get on your nerves. They don't even mean to be your family, they just are.

~ MARSHA NORMAN

The family unit plays a critical role in our society and in the training of the generation to come.

~ SANDRA DAY O'CONNOR

If the family were a fruit, it would be an orange, a circle of sections, held together but separable—each segment distinct.

~ LETTY COTTIN POGREBIN

I've definitely never had to look very far outside my family for inspiration. I'm surrounded by unbelievable strength and courage. Even in very difficult times, there's always been a lot of humor and laughter.

~ MARIA SHRIVER
Interviewed in More *Magazine, May 2004*

You don't choose your family. They are God's gift to you, as you are to them.

~ ARCHBISHOP DESMOND TUTU

Fathers

A QUIET MAN
My father was a quiet man.
His temper calm and mild.
My father was a gentle man
who always wore a smile.
My father was a peaceful man
Who'd never made a row.
A quiet man . . . oh, how I wish.
He could be with me now.

~ ROSALIE FERRER KRAMER
Speaker, poet, author of Dancing in the Dark: Things My Mother Never Told Me
www.authorsden.com/rosaliefkramer

Blessed indeed is the man who hears many gentle voices call him father!

~ LYDIA M. CHILD
Author of Philothea: A Romance, *1836*

Why are men reluctant to become fathers? They aren't through being children.

~ CINDY GARNER

Love and fear. Everything the father of a family says must inspire one or the other.

~ JOSEPH JOUBERT

Fathers represent another way of looking at life—the possibility of an alternative dialogue.

~ LOUISE J. KAPLAN
Author of Oneness and Separateness: From Infant to Individual

Fathers

My father used to play with my brother and me in the yard. Mother would come out and say, "You're tearing up the grass." "We're not raising grass," Dad would reply. "We're raising boys."

~ HARMON KILLEBREW

Never ask for anything that costs more than five dollars when your parents are doing taxes.

~ CARROLAGE 9, *KID'S RULES FOR LIFE*

Don't flush the toilet when your dad's in the shower.

~ LAMAR, AGE 10, KID'S RULES FOR LIFE

Remember you're never too old to hold your father's hand.

~ MOLLY, AGE 11, *KID'S RULES FOR LIFE*

It is much easier to become a father than to be one.

~ KENT NERBURN
Author of Letters to My Son: Reflections on Becoming a Man

Sometimes the poorest man leaves his children the richest inheritance.

~ RUTH E. RENKEL

It is not flesh and blood but the heart which makes us fathers and sons.

~ JOHANN SCHILLER

Most American children suffer too much mother and too little father.

~ GLORIA STEINEM
The New York Times, *26 August 1971*

A father carries pictures where his money used to be.

~ UNKNOWN

Fathers

MY FATHER, THE COWBOY

My father, Douglas Nichols, one of the last real cowboys, was a big strong, proud, hard working and harder drinking Irishman. He was handsome, six foot tall, with broad shoulders, dark hair and piercing blue eyes. I am the youngest of his five children he had with my mother, Helen. He had one son from a previous marriage. Between his first marriage at 20 and second at 36 years old, "Nick" Nichols spent his life between construction all over Texas, gold mines in Colorado, New Mexico State Police and Rodeos. In the Rodeo his event was calf roping. He lived the rough and rowdy life of a real cowboy. He did bit parts in several western movies, riding with the group of horsemen off into the sunset. After he settled down, his interests shifted to shipbuilding in California. He had ideas and would draw pictures of airplane parts. During his forties, his rough-rider days caught up with him. He had back injuries and was stricken with silicosis from gold dust in the lungs. As his disease progressed and he was no longer able to provide for his family; his frustration and bitterness turned to abuse towards my mother and older siblings. As time went on, his disease made him too weak to physically thrust his vengeance, but I remember when he was drunk how he screamed and yelled. I used to take my sister one year older than me with Downs Syndrome and hide in the closet. One night when I was four, I noticed as he started yelling, my teenage brothers and sister scattered out of the house, so I did the same. I ran away down the street and hid under a bush. Later, when I heard one of my brothers calling for me, I came out. I think my mother finally stood up to my father, for making her baby run away from home, and I don't remember him yelling much after that.

When he wasn't drinking, he was a good daddy. I was his baby and he had time to spend with me and he used to teach me. Before I was five, he taught me reading, writing, counting and adding. When I was 8 years old, he succumbed to silicosis and scirosis of the liver at 56 years old. After he passed away, I became keenly aware that no one was going to take care of me; I had to take care of myself. One of my brothers, Jack, stepped in as my mentor and provided life and career guidance. I grew up very independent and luckily met a wonderful, gentle man, Jagdish, whom I married. We now have three grown daughters (Jeena, Jaclyn and Jashree) raised in a peaceful, loving environment.

The purpose of this story is to demonstrate that even from the most difficult origins, if one takes the best from each contribution to their life, with a good attitude they can change their life and succeed. When I think about my father, I know he would be proud that I became an Aerospace Engineer. His contributions to my life were his strong, intelligent genes and nurturing. I think he knew his days were numbered so he tried to teach me all he could. When I catch one of those old western movies, I remind myself that I got the best that ol' cowboy had to offer and I have succeeded. Yes, I am lucky, for my father, the cowboy.

~ JUDY TEJWANI

DADDY'S HANDS

Daddy's hands seemed so still as he lay in his coffin. Callused and gnarled from years of hard work, those strong hands had become the symbol of his enduring love for us all. He was a mountain of man, strong like an ox, a gentle giant, our protector, provider, our bigger-than-life papa bear.

Daddy could lift his three girls off the ground at one time with his little finger while hugging his two boys and our Mom with his free

Fathers <small>CONTINUED</small>

arm. There was nothing on the ranch that he couldn't fix. His desk was constantly littered with a broken toy or trinket that one of his progeny had begged him to repair. There was so much love in those hands. So many wonderful memories were being buried on that bleak December day.

Never at any time in my life had I known such utter and complete desolation. I walked to the pulpit to speak the final farewell for the father I had loved so profoundly. Daddy had asked me to give him a "proper send-off," and I was honored to remember the man who had formed the foundation of my life. As I reminisced about his decades of service to his family and friends, it was Daddy's hands that were the focus of my eulogy. Daddy's hands . . .

Those hands had sacrificed to keep food on the table and a roof over our heads. They had consoled us when we were sad and congratulated us when we accomplished even small feats. Those hands had embraced us, protected us, nurtured us. They had toiled in the vineyards and been scarred by my nails as they gently helped me through my first childbirth. Now they were motionless, slumbering in eternity.

Daddy's hands . . . a symbol of unconditional love lives on in my heart.

~ CYNTHIA BRIAN

Speaker, author of the New York Times *best-selling* Chicken Soup for the Gardener's Soul, Be the Star You Are!, The Business of Show Business *and others. www.star-style.com. From* The Power of Positive Parenting—Daddy's Hands, Mommy's Heart, Children's Memories. ©*2005 Cynthia Brian*

Finding Love

Perhaps after all our worries and questions, we'll discover that all along God had the right thing at the right time for us. Perhaps His plan is more wonderful than anything we could create by ourselves—whether it comes with "pomp and blare," or quietly, "like an old friend." Perhaps ... perhaps ... we should entrust our questions of "How?" and "Who?" and "When?" into His tender care.

~ FROM THE MOVIE *BOY MEETS GIRL*

My dear child, what you must try to see is that nothing has changed. When the Maker brings you your husband, you'll be aware that it was He who made you for each other and He who planned your meeting. And in that moment, just as we did, you'll want to sing a song of praise to Him.

~ FROM THE MOVIE *BOY MEETS GIRL*

A moment like this, some people wait a lifetime for a moment like this. Some people search forever for that one special kiss.
Oh, I can't believe it's happening to me!
Some people wait a lifetime for a moment like this.

~ KELLY CLARKSON
American Idol *winner, song lyrics*

... It is in the touching of one with another that we become most fully ourselves.

~ REVEREND MARILYN DEWLL

This kind of certainty comes, but once in a lifetime.

~ CLINT EASTWOOD
From the movie Bridges of Madison County

Finding Love continued

If you want love, then faithfully, practice living the principles of love
. . . work on yourself and no one else. . . . You know it's love when
the everyday things surrounding you (the leaves, the shade of light
in the sky, a bowl of strawberries) suddenly shimmer with a kind of
unreality.

~ JOAN GATTUSO
Author of A Course in Love

Something very magical takes place in our relationships; our hearts
are filled with the warm glow of forgiveness and inspired by a new
sense of power to realize our hopes and dreams.

~ JOHN GRAY
Author of the Men are From Mars, Women are from Venus *books*

Relationships born out of desperation, seldom last longer than relationships fashioned out of despair.

~ TAMIKA HASKINS

I am looking for someone, who can take as much as I give, give back
as much as I need, and still have the will to live. I am intense, I am in
need, I am in pain, I am in love.

~ SONG LYRICS BY THE INDIGO GIRLS

I am not good at dating. I am a terminal romantic. I resent the distance between "Hello" and "I love you!"

~ BECKY PALMER, AGE 52, NEVER MARRIED

Never be afraid to feel love . . . be afraid of not feeling it.

~ SHELLY PRICE

Finding Love

What do they have to do to make a girl notice them? Guys have to realize that they have to be sweet, caring, gentle, honest and still have that sweet little thing about them that drives any girl crazy: and that's reaching her heart. No matter how much you try, if you don't reach her heart, it won't ever be worthwhile.

~ TARA RZENTKOWSKI

It's funny how we set qualifications for the person to love, when at the back of our minds we know that the one we'll truly love will always be an exception.

~ UNKNOWN

I chased after love for what seemed forever, but it was when I stopped to take a rest that it found me.

~ EILEEN F. WADEL

Somewhere out there is the man you're supposed to marry and if you don't get him first, somebody else will . . . and then, you'll have to spend the rest of your life thinking that somebody else is married to your husband.

~ FROM THE MOVIE *WHEN HARRY MET SALLY*

If it is meant to be, our hearts will find each other when we meet. And if our hearts melt together so will our bodies and souls. Then every word and every touch will fuel our passion flame. I will be yours, you will be mine, and we will be one.

~ CHESTER WRIGHT

Finding Love CONTINUED

Our soulmate is the one who makes life come to life.

~ RICHARD BACH
author of Jonathan Livingston Seagull

Are we not like two volumes of one book?

~ MARCELINE DESBORDES-VALMORE

Soulmates are people who bring out the best in you.
They are not perfect but are always perfect for you.

~ UNKNOWN

Soulmates are locked at the heart and written in the heavens,
promised to find one another when the time is right.

~ UNKNOWN

FINDING LOVE

There's an old legend that the man who catches the garter and the woman who catches the bouquet at a wedding will be the next to marry and may even marry each other.

My dad, Ray Pound, a wedding photographer for over 30 years, was giving the Father of the Groom toast at my wedding eleven years ago. "Now in all my years as a photographer, I never heard of it coming true. However . . ." I squeezed my bride's hand. We smiled at each other as that day thirteen months earlier came back to me with a flash.

My friend Jack was marrying his long-time girlfriend Marlene and invited me to the wedding. Jack was a member of my writing seminar led by Sol Stein (of New York publishing house Stein & Day) and we had become good friends as we learned the finer points of writing craft.

Finding Love <small>CONTINUED</small>

Jack and Marlene had a small wedding in the back yard of their home in Irvine, California on a fine Saturday afternoon in early April. Marlene walked down the aisle and they exchanged vows and rings, kissed as they were declared husband and wife and led us indoors for the reception.

I remember the rituals of the day, the cake cutting, toasts, lots of conversation with friends and finally, the garter toss. Jack wound up and sent the garter high into the air. I lunged forward and to my surprise caught it.

As I relished my success, I felt a tap on my shoulder and turned to see a well-dressed, good-looking woman behind me. "Hi," she said. "I'm Sheri. I caught the bouquet. Maybe we should check this out."

I laughed and we started talking. The party seemed to fade away as we started to get acquainted. Later my friend Steve, also a writing group member, said he came up to us to say something but Sheri and I seemed so engrossed that he moved on to someone else.

We started dating and by September were making wedding plans for the following May 1.

My dad continued his toast while we grinned at the crowd of guests at our wedding. " . . . it happened to these two wonderful people being married today. May they have a long and happy life together."

We will celebrate our eleventh anniversary as we continue our adventures together.

~ LELAND E. POUND
Speaker, Writing Coach, www.leepound.com

Forgiveness

Without forgiveness life is governed by . . . an endless cycle of resentment and retaliation.
~ ROBERTO ASSAGIOLI

Once a woman has forgiven her man, she must not reheat his sins for breakfast.
~ MARLENE DIETRICH

The weak can never forgive. Forgiveness is the attribute of the strong.
~ MAHATMA GANDHI

There's no point in burying a hatchet if you're going to put up a marker on the site.
~ SYDNEY HARRIS

We come here to learn the lessons of forgiveness and self-love.
~ LOUISE HAY
Speaker, author of Empowering Women

Forgive all who have offended you, not for them, but for yourself.
~ HARRIET NELSON

Forgiveness is the final form of love.
~ REINHOLD NIEBUHR
American theologian, 1892–1971

The practice of forgiveness is our most important contribution to the healing of the world.
~ MARIANNE WILLIAMSON
Speaker, author

Flowers & Gardens

FRAGRANT MEMORIES OF WORLD WAR II
In a shady corner where little grew, I planted a gardenia bush.
Thrilled when it bloomed, I plucked the first blossom,
Pressed its sweetness to my face, inhaled and wept.
Suddenly remembering dancing at Sweet Sixteen parties,
And at proms, while overseas there was killing and starvation.

We stacked those Gardenias, in clear boxes, on refrigerator shelves,
Where they browned and withered a few days later.
We danced and laughed with the boys who went away,
Some never to return, just passing from our lives like fragrant corsages.
Yet we went on dancing and smiling.

Those are the memories that flooded my heart,
Spilling tears upon my face, along with the morning dew,
As I plucked the first blossom from my gardenia bush.
The joy of the moment forfeited when I remembered what was lost
While we danced.

~ ROSALIE FERRER KRAMER
Speaker, poet, author of Dancing in the Dark: Things My Mother Never Told Me
www.authorsden.com/rosaliefkramer

Let no one think that real gardening is a bucolic and meditative occupation. It is an insatiable passion, like everything else to which a man gives his heart.

~ KAREL ČAPEK
The Gardener's Year, *translated by M. and R. Weatherall*

A bit of fragrance always clings to the hand that gives roses.

~ CHINESE PROVERB

Flowers & Gardens CONTINUED

Each flower is a soul opening out to nature.

~ GÉRARD DE NERVAL

Gardens are a form of autobiography.

~ SYDNEY EDDISON
Horticulture *magazine, August/September 1993*

Earth laughs in flowers.

~ RALPH WALDO EMERSON
Hamatreya, *a poem*

I've moved cities 6 times, countries and continents 3 times and always it has been the creation of a garden that has settled and calmed. Whether it is the gift of growing, the creation of something new, or the claiming of a space, I am not sure. But for me, gardening has been an essential part of re-establishment and of finding myself.

~ ANNE FRODSHAM
International horticulturist

Science, or para-science, tells us that geraniums bloom better if they are spoken to. But a kind word every now and then is really quite enough. Too much attention, like too much feeding, and weeding and hoeing, inhibits and embarrasses them.

~ VICTORIA GLENDINNING

I'd rather have roses on my table than diamonds on my neck.

~ EMMA GOLDMAN

The kiss of the sun for pardon,
The song of the birds for mirth,
One is nearer God's heart in a garden
Than anywhere else on earth.

~ DOROTHY FRANCES GURNEY
Garden Thoughts, *a poem*

Perfumes are the feelings of flowers.

~ HEINRICH HEINE
The Hartz Journey, *a poem*

Gardening is about enjoying the smell of things growing in the soil, getting dirty without feeling guilty, and generally taking the time to soak up a little peace and serenity.

~ LINDLEY KARSTENS
www.NoProblemGarden.com

Bread feeds the body, indeed, but flowers feed also the soul.

~ *THE KORAN*

When you take a flower in your hand and really look at it, it's your world for the moment.

~ GEORGIA O'KEEFFE

Don't wear perfume in the garden—unless you want to be pollinated by bees.

~ ANNE RAVER

You can bury a lot of troubles digging in the dirt.

~ UNKNOWN

Flowers & Gardens CONTINUED

THOU ART OF FLOWERS

Thou of Flowers,
The fairest and the sweetest that was ever formed
By the God of nature, art to me
The dearest of all my friends.
The rose that is loved by all persons
For its beauty, its grandeur, its sweetness
Cannot vie with the fairness of thy face.

Thou art beautiful
Thy form is perfect
Thy smile is loving and like sunshine.
It gives great joy to those disheartened
It gives great comfort
To them that are mourning.
Sweet is thy face, thy smile, but thou art more
May God who raised thee,
Formed thee and brought thee up
Bless and guide thee through the years to come,
And when thou, flower fairest fadest,
May thou be crowned in heaven
With the crown of life through eternity.

~ FELIX WIJESINGHE JAYEWARDENE
Grand uncle of Dilip Abayasekara

Friendship

TO OUR SPECIAL FRIENDS
You are the persons upon whom we call,
If we're in need of anything at all.
You are the ones who know what to do,
When we feel frightened or just simply blue.
Your compassion has gone a long way,
In helping us get through many a day.
Friendships like yours are simple to define.
They are better than the finest of wines.
So thank you for being there to the end.
It means so much more than you comprehend.

~ ROSALIE FERRER KRAMER
Speaker, poet, author of Dancing in the Dark: Things My Mother Never Told Me
www.authorsden.com/rosaliefkramer

What is a friend? A single soul dwelling in two bodies.

~ ARISTOTLE

There is nothing I would not do for those who are really my friends.
I have no notion of loving people by halves.

~ JANE AUSTIN

A friend is someone you can be alone with and have nothing to do
and not be able to think of anything to say and be comfortable in the
silence.

~ SHERYL CONDIE

I have learned that to have a good friend is the purest of all God's gifts,
for it is a love that has no exchange of payment.

~ FRANCES FARMER

Friendship CONTINUED

The most beautiful discovery true friends make is that they can grow separately without growing apart.
~ ELISABETH FOLEY

Laugh and the world laughs with you. Cry and you cry with your girlfriends.
~ LAURIE KUSLANSKY

In a friend you find a second self.
~ ISABELLE NORTON

The best way to mend a broken heart is time and girlfriends.
~ GWYNETH PALTROW

A friend knows the song in my heart and sings it to me when my memory fails.
~ DONNA ROBERTS

I often think of you and wonder where you are . . . and just sprinkle love out there—knowing that it will find you!
~ SHERYL ROUSH
Speaker, author of Sparkle-Tudes! *and* Heart of A Mother, *www.SparklePresentations.com*

In everyone's life, at some time, our inner fire goes out. It is then burst into flame by an encounter with another human being. We should all be thankful for those people who rekindle the inner spirit.
~ ALBERT SCHWEITZER

Friendship CONTINUED

I am so very blessed to have the love of great friends who continuously remind me that the best part of me is yet to come.

~ CATHERINE TILLEY
Founder of the Institute for Global Healing and Publisher of WISE Publications
www.theglobalvoice.com

Friends are kisses blown to us by angels.

~ UNKNOWN

A true friend reaches for your hand and touches your heart.

~ UNKNOWN

Friends are those rare people who ask how you are and then wait for the answer.

~ UNKNOWN

A friend can tell you things you don't want to tell yourself.

~ FRANCES WARD WELLER

Lots of people want to ride with you in the limo, but what you want is someone who will take the bus with you when the limo breaks down.

~ OPRAH WINFREY

Surround yourself with only people who are going to lift you higher.

~ OPRAH WINFREY

A good friend is a connection to life—a tie to the past, a road to the future, the key to sanity in a totally insane world.

~ LOIS WYSE

Fulfill Your Heart's Desire

Have you ever had one of those moments—when life forces you to take a close look inside your heart and soul? Yes, this is when you begin to discover your true answers.

What answers do you hear when you listen to your heart? I can tell you they are not answers rooted in fear, doubt, worry or lack. They are answers anchored in love, possibility, hope, faith, belief and authentic desire.

Don't wait until you "know it all" before you start to fulfill your heart's desire, because chances are, you'll never know enough. Get started on your dreams; trust the Universe to show you and teach you what you need to be successful. When you truly listen and follow your heart and have a clear vision of how you'll serve others, the Universe comes to help you in miraculous ways.

Trust your heart. Ask for its input and how it feels about a decision and then let it guide you. Whatever you dream of is yours for the asking. This is not to say it will be handed to you on a silver platter. But, it will be given to you if you maintain faith and continue to be guided by your true desire.

Your heart is your compass; let it point you in the direction of your dreams.

~ CHRISTINE KLOSER
Speaker, author, founder of Network for Empowering Women
www.InspirationToRealization.com
Excerpt from Inspiration to Realization: Real Women Reveal Proven Strategies for Personal, Business, Financial and Spiritual Fulfillment
© *2004 Reprinted with Permission*

God

It is this belief in a power larger than myself and other than myself which allows me to venture into the unknown and even the unknowable.

~ MAYA ANGELOU

People see God every day, they just don't recognize him.

~ PEARL BAILEY

When I stand before God at the end of my life, I would hope that I would not have a single bit of talent left, and could say, "I used everything you gave me."

~ ERMA BOMBECK

Some of God's greatest gifts are unanswered prayers.

~ GARTH BROOKS, SINGER, SONG LYRICS

Every evening I turn my worries over to God. He's going to be up all night anyway.

~ MARY C. CROWLEY

See God in every person, place, and thing, and all will be well in your world.

~ LOUISE L. HAY

When the heart and mind are truly open, I can remember to hear with God's ears, speak with His tongue, and see with His eyes. My ears will not hear through my fear, I will not speak from my fear, nor will I see you in the light of my fear. It will be with love.

~ STEPHANIE MOLES
www.TheWoman'sHeart.org

God CONTINUED

Be willing to believe in a greater way about yourself. Let your heart be receptive to God's Spirit and guidance. Have the courage to make the decision to allow the possibility of greatness in you. Take risks beyond your boundaries, and God is right there with you.

~ MARY MANIN MORRISSEY
Author of Life Keys

I know God will not give me anything I can't handle. I just wish that He didn't trust me so much.

~ MOTHER TERESA

Give God full permission.

~ MOTHER TERESA

Prayer is when you talk to God; Meditation is when you listen to God.

~ DIANA ROBINSON

What you are is God's gift to you. What you become is your gift to God.

~ ELEANOR ROOSEVELT

The soul can split the sky in two and let the face of God shine through.

~ EDNA ST. VINCENT MILLAY

God does not ask about our ability, but our availability.

~ UNKNOWN

HEART OF A WOMAN ◆ 89

God CONTINUED

The spiritual meaning of love is measured by what it can do.
Love is meant to heal. Love is meant to renew.
Love is meant to bring us closer to God.

~ UNKNOWN

God understands our prayers
even when we can't find the words to say them.

~ UNKNOWN

You can tell the size of your God by looking at the size of your worry
list. The longer your list, the smaller your God.

~ UNKNOWN

What God intended for you goes far beyond anything you can
imagine.

~ OPRAH WINFREY

Our deepest fear is not that we are inadequate. Our deepest fear is
that we are powerful beyond measure. It is our light, not our darkness,
that frightens us most. We ask ourselves, "Who am I to be brilliant,
gorgeous, talented, and famous?" Actually, who are you not to be?
You are a child of God. Your playing small does not serve the world.
There is nothing enlightened about shrinking so that people won't
feel insecure around you. We were born to make manifest the glory of
God that is within us. It's not just in some of us; it's in all of us. And
when we let our own light shine, we unconsciously give other people
permission to do the same. As we are liberated from our own fear, our
presence automatically liberates others.

~ MARYANNE WILLIAMSON
Used by Nelson Mandela in his 1994 inaugural speech

Grandfathers

Another name for Love—Grandpa, Pappa, Pappy . . .

SOME WORDS NEVER DIE
The words of my Grandfather
Were the words of my Father
And those are the words that are mine
And my words will be the words of my son
And although fathers often say them
It's the young that never seem to hear them.
Or do they?
And its with this knowledge we pass them on.
Sometimes we have to stop and listen
To hear that we were heard.

~ CHRIS GREGORY

GIFTS FROM GRANDPA

I found myself standing in front of the village spread out on the coffee table. Every Christmas since I can remember, Grandma Kate put the village out for our arrival. Mom had always chided me to not touch the pieces, "They're Grandma Kate's special gifts from Grandpa," but this year I seemed to be drawn to them. I bent down to look at one of the pieces more closely. It was Grandma Kate's house and our '87 Chevy wagon was sitting in the driveway. Even the big tree in the front yard was there. My ten-year-old curiosity was reeling. Then something else caught my eye. I held it up for a better view. There, getting out of the car were me and my mom and dad. Grandma was coming across the front lawn to meet us. They looked just like us, right down to my mom's curly red hair caught in mid-bounce and the smile on Grandma's face. It looked like today when we got here.

"Elizabeth Kate!" mom yelped as she walked back into the room. As my name came out of her mouth, I spun, the piece flying out of my hands and across the floor to land at Grandma's feet. "This one came this morning," Grandma's raspy contralto voice became a gravelly sob from within her soul. "Every Christmas Eve since Grandpa and I got married, a piece has arrived at the front door with a note attached, "To Elizabeth Kate with all my love, Sam." After Grandpa died, the pieces kept coming. This one was extra special because Grandpa and I got married 50 years ago tomorrow. This had always been our home and it was the only piece needed to complete the village." Mom tried to comfort her, but no words seemed to help ease her pain.

I cried and heaved in gulps of air as I watched Grandma Kate shrivel into a whimpering child. Dad bent down to pick up the piece with his large hand. He cupped it tenderly and gently placed it back upon the coffee table. I looked at the piece as he set it down. I gasped, "Our car and the big tree are missing!" We searched for several minutes before we found our Chevy wagon and the tree. "Dad, Grandma is missing, too! She was right here," I groaned as I pointed to the spot where her image had been. We searched for several minutes, but we couldn't find the piece that looked like Grandma Kate. When I thought my heart was going to break, I ran to her and buried my face in her apron. She hugged me tight then sat down on the edge of the sofa to cradle me in her arms. "There, there, darlin,' don't fret. It was only a piece of wood." "But it looked just like today when we got here," I sobbed. "You looked so happy." "Yes, it did. But I think we're going to have many more of those happy days, and a funny piece of wood can't replace that."

Her voice was velvety and thick like a swallow of good scotch. My wrenching sobs were cooed to a whimper. My brain couldn't grasp the idea that the piece was irreplaceable, so I never thought another

Grandfathers CONTINUED

thing about it. That is until today when I received a call from Mom that Grandma Kate was in the hospital. I rushed home and brushed open the door. There on the table were the village pieces. I stopped as I saw the broken piece and relived the day I broke it becoming again that ten-year-old child. The past twelve years interrupted my sadness as I looked up and saw the pictures of my own family on the mantle. I turned to leave for the hospital and spotted an envelope lying on the floor. "Lisa" was scrawled on it.

> Dear Lisa,
> You probably don't remember me, but I'm the man who asked your dad to come take over the lumberyard when you were a child. I want someone to know the story of the village pieces.
> Before your Grandpa Sam died, he asked me to continue making them if anything ever happened to him. "The last one," he had said, "will be our home with my daughter and her family. Deliver it on Christmas Eve before our 50th wedding anniversary." I just wanted someone to know.

He simply signed the note "Roy Brown."

My heart sank as I remembered my mom's words, "They're special gifts from Grandpa." Indeed they were. I went to the hospital to see Grandma Kate. I read her the note from Mr. Brown. She smiled, squeezed my hand, closed her eyes, and slipped away. I know she gave Grandpa a kiss when she saw him for each of her special gifts.

~ LINDA ULRICH

Grandmothers

Names for Love—Grandma, Nana, Yah-yah, Oma, Gran, Nannie . . .

WHAT ARE GRANDMAS FOR?
Grandmas are for stories about things of long ago.
Grandmas are for caring about all the things you know.
Grandmas are for rocking you and singing you to sleep.
Grandmas are for giving you nice memories to keep.
Grandmas are for knowing all the things you're dreaming of.
But, most of all, Grandmas are for love.

~ UNKNOWN

WHAT IS A GRANDMA?
A grandma is warm hugs and sweet memories.
She remembers all of your accomplishments
and forgets all of your mistakes.
She is someone you can tell your secrets and worries to,
And she hopes and prays that all your dreams come true.
She always loves you, no matter what.
She can see past temper tantrums and bad moods,
And makes it clear that they don't affect how precious you are to her.
She is an encouraging word and a tender touch.
She is full of proud smiles.
She is the one person in the world who loves you with all her heart,
Who remembers the child you were
and cherishes the person you've become.

~ BARBARA CAGE

Grandmothers CONTINUED

Grandparents bestow upon their grandchildren
The strength and wisdom that time
And experience have given them.
Grandchildren bless their Grandparents
With a youthful vitality and innocence
That help them stay young at heart forever.
Together they create a chain of love
Linking the past with the future.
The chain may lengthen,
But it will never part . . .

~ UNKNOWN

✦ ✦ ✦

Ever since the day I was born.
You have nurtured me with love and kindness.
You have been someone I can believe in,
And someone I can depend upon.
In this world I am just starting to understand.
And it's important to me that you know
How grateful that I am,
For all that you give to me,
For all that you teach me,
And for the strength I will always have,
Because of you, grandma.

~ UNKNOWN

Grandmothers CONTINUED

GRANDMA'S GONE COMPUTER

In the not too distant past—I remember very well—
Grandmas tended to their knitting and their cookies were just swell.
They were always at the ready when you needed some advice.
And their sewing (I can tell you) was available—and nice.
Well, Grandma's not deserted you, she dearly love you still . . .
You just won't find her cooking, but she's right there at the till.
She thinks about you daily—you haven't been forsook.
Your photos are quite handy in the Pentium notebook.
She scans your art work now though and combines it with cool sound,
To make electronic greetings. She prints pictures by the pound.
She's right there when you need her, you really aren't alone,
She's out now with her "puter pals," but she took her new cell phone.
You can also leave a message on her answering machine;
Or page her at the fun meet, she's been there since eight fifteen.
Yes, the world's a very different place, there is no doubt of that.
So "E" her from her web page, or join her in a chat.
She's joined the electronic age and it really seems to suit her.
So don't expect the same old gal, cause Grandma's gone "Computer!"

~ UNKNOWN

Grandmothers CONTINUED

MY FIRST GRANDCHILD

When I picked up Jackie she smiled
a crooked toothless grin.
She made great yawn,
And I melted.
Holding close the black fuzzy haired
Facsimile of her mother,
I knew that nothing would ever
Be the same again.
That loving cannot be told in words,
It just flows back and forth,
Between us . . . never stopping,
Like the tide.
This is my first grandchild,
She's the pride of my life,
And the joy of my world.
A truly exceptional baby.

~ ROSALIE FERRER KRAMER
Speaker, poet, author, www.authorsden.com/rosaliefkramer

MY SECOND GRANDCHILD

Our Dayna is something like a rash,
That tickles where you cannot scratch.
She turned somersaults on the floor,
But smashed into the kitchen door.
She has a certain brand of kisses,
Sticky and wet and so delicious,
That thoughts of discipline turn to ashes,
When blue eyes peek through long black lashes.
Pretending is her favorite game.
A bunny, a kitten—never the same.
Angel, puppy, a bird in flight,
A chicken, a dancer, big red kite.
She entered life in second place.
Yet fills for me a special space.
Like moon and stars or sunny day
She lights my life in every way.

~ ROSALIE FERRER KRAMER
Speaker, poet, author, www.authorsden.com/rosaliefkramer

Grandmothers CONTINUED

GRANDMA'S HUGS ARE MADE OF LOVE

Everything my grandma does is something special made with love.
She takes me to add the extra touch that says, "I love you very much."
She fixes hurts with a kiss and smile and
tells good stories grandma-style.
It's warm and cozy on her lap for secret telling or a nap.
And when I say my prayers at night
I ask God to bless and hold her tight.
Cause when it comes to giving hugs
my grandma's arms are filled with love.

~ UNKNOWN

GIFTS FROM GRANDMOTHER

In May of 2002, I received my Bachelors Degree. This ceremony was put into motion seventy years ago. My grandmother had earned a scholarship for college. Societal norms dictated that she relinquish it. Few women of color attended college in the 1930s. My mother's generation continued the dream of higher action. Financial difficulties and having children slowed the process. The love and wisdom of two generations of women laid the foundation for my degree. I was the first female in the family to receive a Bachelors. I am thankful for their shoulders that I climbed upon to reach this goal. From the smiles on their faces, it was clear that we all graduated that day.

~ RENEE CARTER, SPEAKER

Gratitude & Happiness

Gratitudes are actions you can take that refine your ability to distinguish between the world of fear and the world of freedom, between fear-based feelings and your freedom-based intuition. When you consciously choose to see the good that is already present in your life, you immediately open up the floodgates for more good to come your way.

~ RHONDA BRITTEN
Speaker, author of Fearless Living

An attitude of gratitude is to prosperity what sunshine is to flowers.

~ BETTY COLSTON

Gratitude is the heart's memory.

~ FRENCH PROVERB

I'm fulfilled in what I do . . . I never thought that a lot of money or fine clothes—the finer things of life—would make you happy. My concept of happiness is to be filled in a spiritual sense.

~ CORETTA SCOTT KING

Acting happier than you feel can make you happier than you are.

~ FRAN LEBOWITZ

The more you praise and celebrate your life, the more there is in life to celebrate.

~ OPRAH WINFREY

Health

In one day:
Your heart will likely beat over 100,000 times
Your blood will travel about 168,000 miles
You will breathe about 23,000 times
You will eat over three pounds of food
You will drink three pounds of liquids
You will turn in your sleep 25–30 times
You may speak about 48,000 words
You will use some 7,000,000 brain cells

Never go to a doctor whose office plants have died.
~ ERMA BOMBECK

Pampering is preventative medicine,
not a recuperative strategy after crashing.
~ BETH BURNS
Professional life coach, www.BrightSideCoaching.com

Seasonal foods nourish us, through tradition and warm remembrances, and fortify our bodies. Cooking with foods of the season allows us to enjoy foods when they are most flavorful, the brightest in color, and most abundant in juice and texture—when they are perfect gifts from nature. They need little adornment or fatty sauces.
~ LESA HEEBNER
Speaker, author of Cooking with the Seasons

Dear Mr. God,
I wish you would not make it so easy for people to come apart.
I had to have 3 stitches and a shot.
~ JANET, *KID'S THEOLOGY*

Health CONTINUED

The more enthusiasm you have, the healthier you feel and the faster you heal, whether you're recovering from an illness, accident, broken heart, death of a loved one, end of a marriage, or any other type of loss. Research has now proven that laughter, optimism, and a will to live—all aspects of enthusiasm—speed up healing time and increase well-being and longevity.

~ MARY MARCDANTE
Speaker, author, www.MaryMarcdante.com

I am radiantly beautiful, vibrantly healthy, extraordinarily creative, abundantly wealthy, and full of boundless energy, joy and awe!

~ DIANNE ONSTAD
Co-author of ABC's of YES! ~Actions For Prosperity, *www.MagicOfYes.com*

Chronic diseases on the rise like high blood pressure, Type 2 diabetes (high blood sugar) and high cholesterol all respond favorably to positive lifestyle change such as the addition of regular exercise and the consumption of more fruits and vegetables daily. We have the power to motivate ourselves toward positive change every day. Thus the quote, "If something changes, then something changes."

~ MARY ROUSH, RN, CDE
Patient educator of Kauai Medical Clinic

Heart disease continues to be the #1 cause of death in the U.S. I believe this is because we are a society of broken hearts. Practicing kindness and compassion toward ourselves and one another is one of the best antidotes for heart disease.

~ DIANA WEISS-WISDOM, PH.D.
Author of Stress and A Healthy Ticker: A Psychological Approach to Preventing Heart Disease

Health CONTINUED

QUITTING IS NOT AN OPTION

*I*n my early twenties I was leading a very intense life of working hard and playing hard too. A workaholic at a Vancouver-based advertising and P.R. agency, I was working 10–12 hour days and then playing competitive beach volleyball or training for a triathlon in the evenings. I began noticing that my feet were going numb and over a few months, the numbness turned to a lack of coordination and eventually paralysis of both legs and numbness to my neck when I was hospitalized and diagnosed with Multiple Sclerosis (MS) in 1986.

Twenty years ago the medical profession was unsure of the cause of MS or how to cure it and they're still unsure today. The physicians didn't have any certain explanations of what the results/outcome of the disease would be other than probable fatigue, possible recurring or permanent paralysis and/or blindness. The roller coaster of emotions which I felt I needed to hide from others ranged from confusion to fear. The confusion was about the uncertainty of how my career and life would evolve. The fear was that I might not be able to continue the fast paced life, athletics and international travel I enjoyed so very much. The other unexpected feeling was motivation which was the strongest driving force as I have always believed that I had no limitations on achieving success.

I was fueled by the challenge of proving that the MS was not going to limit my life. After giving my employer six months notice that I was resigning, I opened my own Event Marketing & Communications agency. My client list included several of Canada's largest corporations and as my company grew, so did the progression of the MS symptoms with relapsing-remitting attacks of paralysis or blindness. Each attack varied in length and severity, occurring every 8–10 months apart for the next decade. I'm sure the attacks were harder on my staff and business partner than they were on me.

In 1997 when Princess Diana died, I was asked to co-produce an event as a tribute to her life and the charities she supported. The event involved three symphony orchestras and the cruelest irony struck on my way to the gala evening when I was involved in a head-on collision! Imagine, on my way to a tribute for a woman killed in a car accident and I was nearly killed by a drunk driver. The whiplash and injuries triggered a severe and acute MS attack that left me unable to stand or walk on my own for nearly four months. Having an amazing team of employees who carried the load while I attempted to recover, I hired a personal trainer to try work out my limp legs, which had atrophied from not being used for several months. He suggested I begin a potent regime of antioxidants and he recommended pharmaceutical-grade products from USANA Health Sciences.

After extensive research, I made a commitment to a holistic healing approach that would include diet, exercise and a number of their nutritional supplements. At that time I was using a walker for support and shared with one of my medical advisors my desire to regain my ability to walk, to resume running my company (which my staff were managing) and to eventually eliminate prescription medications. In only a few months, I parked the walker and wheelchair and my belief in the importance of nutritional supplements became unshakable as I was able to eliminate prescription drugs within one year. Prior to the car accident I had been having an MS attack that was either paralyzing or blinding at 8–10 month intervals for eleven years. I am pleased to say that it has now been seven years since my last MS attack. I still have MS, but the symptoms are dramatically reduced.

My life is still very full and includes international travel with my husband, Martin. On a recent trip to Greece, I climbed the stairs of the Acropolis (something that I was told could never happen when I was hospitalized!). There we were, my husband following behind me

Health continued

carrying a wheelchair in case I tired and humming the theme from "Rocky" as I climbed all the way to the top! Quitting has never been an option for me. I've also recently become a golf enthusiast and when people ask what my golf handicap is, I answer "which one" because I have letters AND numbers as my response!

I emphasize the importance of "an attitude of gratitude" and not taking our health for granted. It's amazing how much more beautiful a sunset looks after you've lost your eyesight for a week or how wonderful a walk on the beach is when you've been in a wheelchair for several months.

I even saw the silk-lining in having my legs go numb—during the severe MS attacks it turned out to be an ideal time to have them waxed! Now, my life is about finding new and creative ways to accept and work with the limitations I have for today while continuing to contribute to others in order to make this a better place for all our tomorrows.

Even though my body sometimes gives me messages to slow down and smell the roses as I walk along the journey of life, above all else, it is important to remember that quitting is not an option.

~ JAN MILLS
www.janmills.net

Editor's Note: Jan was a spokesperson in Vancouver for the MS Society of Canada, and still lectures at various health symposiums. She is passionate about sharing her knowledge of the importance of pharmaceutical grade supplements (USANA) and other complimentary therapies (Sanoviv Medical Institute) as health prevention.

Heart

H—heal your heart
E—exercise your emotions
A—accept your uniqueness
R—relax and trust
T—thankfulness

~ ADELE ALFANO
Author of Expert Women Who Speak . . . Speak Out!

There is nothing enduring in life for a woman except what she builds in a man's heart.

~ JUDITH ANDERSON

When people go to work, they shouldn't have to leave their hearts at home.

~ BETTY BENDER

When your heart speaks, take good notes.

~ JUDITH CAMPBELL

I wear my heart on my sleeve.

~ DIANA, PRINCESS OF WALES

The woman's vision is deep reaching, the man's far reaching. With the man the world is his heart, with the woman the heart is her world.

~ BETTY GRABLE

What we have most to fear is failure of the heart.

~ SONIA JOHNSON

Heartache & Heartbreak

The one who loves you will make you weep.
~ ARGENTIAN PROVERB

When the pain of the present becomes greater
than the fear of the future, change becomes attractive.
~ BETTY COLSTON

When you are sorrowful look again in your heart,
and you shall see that in truth you are weeping
for that which has been your delight.
~ KAHLIL GIBRAN

The tragedy is not that love doesn't last.
The tragedy is the love that lasts.
~ SHIRLEY HAZZARD

What soap is for the body, tears are for the soul.
~ JEWISH PROVERB

God is closest to those with broken hearts.
~ JEWISH PROVERB

Hope is the feeling you have that the feeling you have isn't permanent.
~ JEAN KERR

Maybe I could have loved you better.
Maybe you should have loved me more.
Maybe our hearts were just next in line.
Maybe everything breaks sometime.
~ JEWEL KILCHER, SINGER, SONG LYRICS

Heartache & Heartbreak CONTINUED

Those who do not know how to weep with their whole heart don't know how to laugh either.

~ GOLDA MEIR

It's not easy saying this to you. It's the hardest thing I've ever had to do. But, Boy, before you go, I want you to know . . . I wish you strength, when times are hard. I wish with all my heart you find just what you're lookin' for. I wish you joy. I wish you peace, and that every star you see is within your reach, and I wish you still loved me.

~ JO DEE MESSINA, SONG LYRICS FROM *I WISH*

Have you ever been hurt and the place tries to heal a bit, and you just pull the scar off of it over and over again.

~ ROSA PARKS

The first time my heart was broken I thought I was through; I swore I'd never love again and believe me this was true, but when you walked into my life the second your eyes met mine, I knew you were worth loving, just like before, just like the first time.

~ BECKY RHEAULT

Think of a breakup this way: you're one step closer to the one you're meant to be with.

~ SUBMITTED BY SARAH

There is nothing sadder in this life than to watch someone you love walk away after they have left you. To watch the distance between your two bodies expand until there is nothing left but empty space . . . and silence.

~ FROM THE MOVIE *SOMEONE LIKE YOU*

Heartache & Heartbreak continued

She cried when I left her, now, I cry to forget her. Oh, how foolish I was to ever want to leave because nobody in his right mind would have left her . . . even my heart was smart enough to stay behind.
~ GEORGE STRAIT, SINGER, SONG LYRICS

Maybe part of loving is learning to let go.
~ FROM THE TV SERIES *THE WONDER YEARS*

I never knew until that moment how bad it could hurt to lose something you never really had.
~ FROM THE TV SERIES *THE WONDER YEARS*

I would've loved you anyway;
I'd do it all the same;
not a second I would change,
not a touch that I would trade.
Had I known my heart would break,
I'd've loved you anyway.
~ TRISHA YEARWOOD
Song lyrics from I'd've Loved You Anyway

One day someone will walk into your life, and you will know why it never worked out with anyone else.
~ UNKNOWN

Sometimes I wish I were a little kid again, skinned knees are easier to fix than broken hearts.
~ UNKNOWN

Heartache & Heartbreak

God can heal a broken heart, but He has to have all the pieces.

~ UNKNOWN

Giving up doesn't always mean you are weak; sometimes it means that you are strong enough to let go.

~ UNKNOWN

When love is lost, do not bow your head in sadness; instead keep your head up high and gaze into heaven for that is where your broken heart has been sent to heal.

~ UNKNOWN

Relationships are like glass. Sometimes it's better to leave them broken than try to hurt yourself putting it back together.

~ UNKNOWN

Hobbies

Passion Hobbies

*P*assion Hobbies are pastimes that have significant value, something that we do to nurture our spirit and balance our balance. These are activities that brings us joy, enlighten and center, enrich and empower us. For most of us—it's what we do AFTER work that helps us keep our sanity AT work.

Women in my seminars tell me their favorite passion hobbies include: reading mystery or romance novels; walking, running, or aerobics; making needlepoint and crafts for others; jigsaw and crossword puzzles; doing fun and playful things with their kids; and, of course, shopping makes this list every time! I enjoy gathering my women friends for an evening out dancing! It's great exercise, safe and fun.

All the years growing up, I remember my father would rush home from work and head out to the back yard where he would enjoy his passion hobby—organic gardening. He would take out any of his frustrations, find his inner peace, and then come into the house. I know for him (and for us) it allows time to re-center and re-group from the day, helping him to lead a more balanced life. Today, years after his retirement, it's STILL his passion hobby. A pastime that has nurtured his spirit over the years, and brings a smile every time he shares fresh fruits and vegetables with neighbors, friends and family.

My mother, Beverly Roush, on the other hand, loves to volunteer time to organizations such as the U.S. Olympic Training Center—and received Volunteer of the Year for her time and energy leading tour groups and helping Olympians pack gear for the upcoming events.

What passion hobbies do you currently have in your life—or could to incorporate into your life on a regular basis that will bring you pleasure, spiritual rejuvenation and greater life balance?

~ SHERYL ROUSH

Speaker, author of Sparkle-Tudes! *and* Heart of A Mother, *and contributing author of to* The Princess Principle: Women Helping Women Discover Their Royal Spirit, *www.Sparkle Presentations.com*

Hugs

A hug is a kiss for the soul.
~ KRISTY GAYTAN

A hug is like a boomerang—you get it back right away.
~ BIL KEANE
Family Circus *cartoonist*

Hugging has no unpleasant side effects and is all natural. There are no batteries to replace, it's inflation-proof and non-fattening with no monthly payments. It's non-taxable, non-polluting, and is, of course, fully refundable.
~ UNKNOWN

You can't give a hug without getting a hug.

Sometimes it's better to put love into hugs than to put it into words.

A hug is the shortest distance between friends.

Hug Department: Always Open

You can't wrap love in a box, but you can wrap a person in a hug.

A hug is a handshake from the heart.

Hugs are the universal medicine.

A hug is a great gift—one size fits all, and it's easy to exchange.

A kiss without a hug is like a flower without the fragrance.

Hugs grease the wheels of the world.

I don't discriminate—I'm an equal-opportunity hugger.
~ UNKNOWN

Husbands

If I had known the family I never would have married my husband!
~ NAME INTENTIONALLY DELETED!

Whatever cleanin' goes on on the planet, women do 99% of it. But see, women are not as proud of their 99% as men are of our one! We clean sumpin' up we're gonna talk about it all year long . . . "Look don't worry about emptyin' that ashtray, I done got it alright?
Did it for you, Sweet Pea."
~ JEFF FOXWORTHY

I want a man who's kind and understanding. Is that too much to ask of a millionaire?
~ ZSA ZSA GABOR

A retired husband is often a wife's full-time job.
~ ELLA HARRIS

The old theory was "Marry an older man, because they're more mature." But the new theory is: "Men don't mature. Marry a younger one."
~ RITA RUDNER

If you've got them by the balls their hearts and minds will follow.
~ JOHN "THE DUKE" WAYNE

The only time a woman really succeeds in changing a man is when he is a baby.
~ NATALIE WOOD

"BASTA!"
*Chronicles of the joys of living with the
habits of a spouse after retirement.*

Picture this: Summer, 1970, rows of brick fronted houses with varicolored aluminum trims on a South Philadelphia street, standing shoulder to shoulder like Catholic schoolgirls in uniform, but with jewelry. Lace curtains flapping through open windows in the steamy breeze. It's too hot to run; my shirt is sticking to my back as I walk. Even so, somebody's mother is cooking "red gravy" (marinara.) I'll go home with clothes smelling of garlic and tomato.

"Hello, Nanna," I call to my friend Mona's grandmother. Everybody calls her Nanna. She doesn't answer. She doesn't speak English. She crabwalks to the side of the marble steps she's scrubbing to let me pass.

I came to Mona's to play today, but it's too hot and we're restless. We were horsing around in the parlor (a real no-no), and nearly took out the white plaster Virgin Mary that hangs next to a signed and framed photo of Frank Sinatra. Now we've been caught "finger-painting" in the sweat our legs left on the plastic covered sofa.

"Basta!" Mrs. Ianelli bellows. Forget language barrier. We knew what Mrs. Ianelli meant: You've crossed the line.

Now, thirty years later, it's payback time. Now, I'm ready to bellow, "Basta!"

Picture this: 2002, a stereotypical tree-lined suburban California neighborhood. Nobody's cooked marinara since the discovery of Ragu.™

Ladies, I believe I speak for many of us. Gentlemen: if the shoe fits . . .

Husbands continued

There comes a time when a man is home too much. Too soon. Maybe he's heard the lace-edged euphemism for, "You're outta here." Downsizing, early retirement, whatever.

Willis, my husband, was given the gift of the latter, courtesy of the former. The upshot is: he's underfoot. Constantly. We're buddies; that'd be okay, except for one thing.

Willis used to be a "strategic planner." He could Set Objectives. He could Measure Results. He could Analyze. His first week at home, he wanted to reorganize my kitchen. "Get thee to the garage," I said sweetly. Now we've moved to a condo. No garage. No outside chores.

Willis is tired of reading. "How about woodworking?" I suggest. We have a well-equipped clubhouse. No dice.

He's taken up a new hobby: weather watching. We live in southern California. Weather watching should take ten seconds, tops, a day. But in San Diego, the average temperature is ten degrees hotter every ten miles inland from the coast. So Wally, our local Weather Guy, reports on five different "micro-climates" in the metro area. Twice a day. With five day forecasts for each.

I could live with that. But Willis is also checking two different thermometers here at home. An indoor/outdoor digital, in the shade outside the bedroom, and another in the sun on the patio. And two Internet weather sites. Several times a day. You with me?

Stick your head out the window! I'm thinking. Have I mentioned he rarely leaves our microclime? Another sunny day. Multiple trips to the thermometers and the Internet sites.

Now he's unloading the dishwasher. Good husband, I think, mentally patting him on the head. I can't exactly complain. He's stacking the bowls on the shelf. "Hey," he says, "there's only five bowls here." He looks puzzled. "Where are the other three?"

Husbands CONTINUED

He waits for my horror. I am horrified. He's counting the bowls. Cabinet doors bang open, then slam closed. He's working himself into a frenzy. Over bowls. "Where could they be?" he moans. "They're either here somewhere or they're broken," I venture. We're not talking Limoges china. More cabinet doors slamming.

Here's where the "Basta" comes in. But I hold my tongue. Because he's starting to have an effect on me. Yesterday, I found myself aligning the flowers on the stacked dinner plates. All the flowers should be at the bottom, for ease of table setting, I thought.

And today I feel like playing with his head. I just deliberately slipped a fork in the spoon slot in the drawer. That'll be good for a few minutes of fun! Somebody save me!

~ LYNN MARSHALL GAHMAN

In Sickness & In Health

*M*y wife, Carol, and I had no trouble with the "in health" part during 35 wonderful years together. But, the "in sickness" part was put to the test in a way that we couldn't have imagined when we first uttered those words.

Two years ago, I was diagnosed with a terminal liver disease and was placed on the Federal transplant waiting list. But the disease progressed so quickly that my doctors warned me I wouldn't survive the three to five year wait. My only hope—a partial liver transplant from a living donor.

Carol immediately volunteered—no, make that insisted—on being my donor. She knew it was a risky and painful operation. And the scars would remain for the rest of her life. But her love for me overrode all other concerns.

The simultaneous 12-hour operations went smoothly. However, during recovery I suffered a setback. The doctors worried that I might not make it.

Once again, Carol's love came to the rescue. Fighting the pain and weakness from her own operation, she stayed at my bedside twelve to fourteen hours a day, sometimes more. Love and encouragement poured from her lips as she fought back the tears. She refused to let me die. And the love she demonstrated during those dark days saved my life . . . again.

True love can conquer even death.

~ MELVIN A. CREIGHTON AND CAROL A. CREIGHTON
From the book, The Umbrella, A Love Story
© Copyright 2005. Reprinted with Permission.

Kindness

Too often we underestimate the power of a touch, a smile, a kind word, a listening ear, an honest compliment, or the smallest act of caring, all of which have the potential to turn a life around.

~ LEO BUSCAGLIA

A bit of fragrance always clings to the hand that gives roses.

~ CHINESE PROVERB

There is one word which may serve as a rule of practice for all one's life—reciprocity.

~ CONFUCIUS

The kindness and affection from the public have carried me through some of the most difficult periods, and always your love and affection have eased the journey.

~ DIANA, PRINCESS OF WALES

Whatever you give will find countless ways back to you.

~ DOVE PROMISES CHOCOLATE INSCRIPTION

Being considerate of others will take your children further in life than any college degree.

~ MARIAN WRIGHT EDELMAN

Open your heart—open it wide; someone is standing outside.

~ MARY ENGELBREIT
Believe: A Christmas Treasury

Kindness CONTINUED

As the bus slowed down at the crowded bus stop, the Pakistani bus conductor leaned from the platform and called out, "Six only!" The bus stopped. He counted on six passengers, rang the bell, and then, as the bus moved off, called to those left behind: "So sorry, plenty of room in my heart—but the bus is full." He left behind a row of smiling faces. It's not what you do, it's the way that you do it.

~ FRANCIS GAY
Author of The Friendship Book of Francis Gay

The fruit of the Spirit is love, joy, peace, patience, kindness, goodness, faithfulness.

~ GALATIANS 5:22, WOMEN'S DEVOTIONAL BIBLE 2, NEW INTERNATIONAL VERSION

During my second year of nursing school our professor gave us a quiz. I breezed through the questions until I read the last one: "What is the first name of the woman who cleans the school?" Surely this was a joke. I had seen the cleaning woman several times, but how would I know her name? I handed in my paper, leaving the last question blank. Before the class ended, one student asked if the last question would count toward our grade. "Absolutely," the professor said. "In your careers, you will meet many people. All are significant. They deserve your attention and care, even if all you do is smile and say hello." I've never forgotten that lesson. I also learned her name was Dorothy.

~ JOANN C. JONES

Kindness CONTINUED

I have never met a person whose greatest need was anything other than real, unconditional love. You can find it in a simple act of kindness toward someone who needs help. There is no mistaking love. You feel it in your heart. It is the common fiber of life, the flame that heals our soul, energizes our spirit and supplies passion to our lives. It is our connection to God and to each other.
~ ELIZABETH KUBLER-ROSS

Let no one ever come to you without leaving better and happier. Be the living expression of God's kindness: kindness in your face, kindness in your eyes, kindness in your smile.
~ MOTHER TERESA

A kind word is like a Spring day.
~ RUSSIAN PROVERB

Send loving kindness to yourself, your family, your friends, your community, people near and far and eventually to your enemies. You do not need to go and take care of everyone. Just learn to love them by allowing them to express themselves in their own ways.
~ SANDRA SCHRIFT
Career coach, www.schrift.com

Don't wait for people to be friendly, show them how.
~ UNKNOWN

Kisses

Kissing is like drinking salted water. You drink, and your thirst increases.
~ CHINESE PROVERB

Any man who can drive safely while kissing a pretty girl is simply not giving the kiss the attention it deserves.
~ ALBERT EINSTEIN

You will never know how you feel about someone till you kiss them.
~ FROM THE MOVIE *40 DAYS AND 40 NIGHTS*

'Twas not my lips you kissed . . . But my soul.
~ JUDY GARLAND

Ancient lovers believed a kiss would literally unite their souls, because the spirit was said to be carried in one's breath.
~ EVE GLICKSMAN

You shouldn't kiss me like this, unless you mean it like that . . . "cause I just close my eyes and I won't know where I'm at. We'll get lost on this dance floor, spinning around, and around and around and around. They're all watching us now, they think we're falling in love, they'll never believe we're just friends. You shouldn't kiss me like this unless you mean it like that, but if you do, Baby, kiss me again.
~ TOBY KEITH, SINGER, SONG LYRICS

your kiss
like peanut butter
delights the pallid tongue
~ MARY LENORE QUIGLEY
Author of By Fools Like Me: Heart Songs in Verse

He Kissed Me

When he kissed me that night in the darkness,
Party noises seemed very far away.
I trembled upon hearing his steps behind me,
And felt his arms go 'round my waist.

I did not wish to wake from that dream,
But I couldn't respond for I was afraid.
And I knew that this could never be,
That we must stay, as always, "just friends."

But I have never been quite the same,
Since that night so very long ago,
In that dark and silent room,
When he kissed me, and said, "I love you."

~ ROSALIE FERRER KRAMER
Speaker, poet, author of Dancing in the Dark: Things My Mother Never Told Me
www.authorsden.com/rosaliefkramer

When [he] kisses you he isn't doing anything else. You're his whole universe . . . and the moment is eternal because he doesn't have any plans and isn't going anywhere. Just kissing you . . . it's overwhelming.

~ UNKNOWN

Her kisses left something to be desired . . . the rest of her.

~ UNKNOWN

Friends are kisses blown to us by angels.

~ UNKNOWN

Laughter

If you can laugh at it, you can live with it.
~ ERMA BOMBECK

Humor comes from self-confidence.
~ RITA MAE BROWN

Comedy is tragedy plus time.
~ CAROL BURNETT

Time spent laughing is time spent with the Gods.
~ JAPANESE PROVERB

Remember, men need laughter sometimes more than food.
~ ANNA FELLOWS JOHNSTON

He deserves Paradise who makes his companions laugh.
~ *THE KORAN*

Blessed is she who has learned to laugh at herself for she shall never cease to be entertained.
~ UNKNOWN

A sense of humor is the lubricant of life's machinery.
~ UNKNOWN

If you can look into the mirror without laughter, you have no sense of humor.
~ UNKNOWN

A laugh is a smile that bursts.
~ MARY H. WALDRIP

Learning to Love Yourself

Make your day by becoming and being the person who makes your heart smile.

~ MARIA MARSALA
www.ElevatingYou.com

When you find peace within yourself, you become the kind of person who can live at peace with others.

~ PEACE PILGRIM

You teach people who you are by the way you treat yourself.

~ LYNN PIERCE
Author of Change One Thing, Change Your Life, *www.ChangeOneThing.com*

Be assured that you will always have time for the things you put first.

~ LIANE STEELE

The gift I found in this forever evolving, sometimes rocky yet incredible relationship was me.

~ CATHERINE TILLEY
Founder of the Institute for Global Healing and Publisher of WISE Publications
www.theglobalvoice.com

It isn't until you come to a spiritual understanding of who you are—not necessarily a religious feeling, but deep down, the spirit within—that you can begin to take control.

~ OPRAH WINFREY

Declare today "sacred time"—off-limits to everyone, unless invited by you. Take care of your personal wants and needs. Say no, graciously but firmly, to others' demands.

~ OPRAH WINFREY

Learning to Love Yourself CONTINUED

AFFIRMATIONS FOR HONORING OURSELVES

I am a valued human being.
I am always treated with respect.
I am empowered.
I am supportive of other women.
I easily speak up for myself.
I deserve to have boundaries.
My boundaries are respected.
I make waves whenever I need to.
I have a good support team.
I have integrity.
The more open I am, the safer I am.
I am a woman healing other women.
I have a strong energy barrier.
The men in my life honor women.
I take my power back.
I love and honor myself.

~ LOUISE L. HAY
Author of Empowering Women

LEARNING TO LOVE YOURSELF

Love yourself exactly as you are, and you are forever changed
Love everything you can from wherever you find yourself
Think of someone you love a lot, and love yourself that much
When you forget how to love yourself, love yourself for forgetting
Jump from logic into the safety net of love
Open your love big enough to fit all your feelings
Say, "I can love myself for that" too!
Love others exactly as they are, and they are free to change.

~ KATHLYN & GAY HENDRICKS
Conscious Loving

Learning to Love Yourself

LOVING YOURSELF IS
YOUR SPIRITUAL RIGHT

*O*n a scale of 1 to 10, with 10 being tops, how well do you love yourself? Despite years of education and life experience, most of us fail miserably in loving ourselves. Subtle patterns of assuming guilt, preoccupation with fear, and the many times daily we listen to the inner critic all prevent us from responding to the core of our need for love.

The struggle to love yourself is vital to your well-being. It is time to give yourself the love you deserve—from yourself. In fact, if you loved yourself twice as much right now, how would you do it?

Your list might include lightening your load, giving yourself more comfort, releasing old patterns of thought or action holding you back, practicing more holistic health care, praying for yourself, or simply taking quiet time to meditate.

Loving yourself is not selfish. It is a bold affirmation of the value of your life. It is important to remind yourself that you deserve such love—for better health, a more positive outlook on life, and the ability to contribute to the universe the rich resources within you waiting for Soul escape.

The benefits of loving yourself twice as much are extraordinary. You will be more joyous, satisfied, liberated, empowered, ready to expand and unleash your vast potential, and able to give and receive love at a much higher level.

Learning to Love Yourself CONTINUED

Here are some ways to love yourself twice as much:

- *Go to a private spot that feels like a sanctuary and allow yourself, in utter stillness, to feel the idea of truly loving yourself.*
- *Quietly ask divine Love how you could best love yourself more.*
- *Affirm to yourself: "I know that loving myself acknowledges my oneness with Love. I claim—for myself and all humanity—that we all deserve such inner love honoring."*
- *Post your list of how you plan to love yourself twice as much. Notice how many items on your list do not depend on anyone but you!*
- *Share your list with a friend or loved one.*
- *Practice loving yourself more each day. Remember, transformation begins with a single step.*

—DR. SCOTT PECK & SHANNON PEC
Co-founders of TheLoveCenter, a non-profit educational organization dedicated to bringing all humanity into the heart of Love. They are co-authors of The Love You Deserve, Liberating Your Magnificence.
©Copyright 2001Scott & Shannon Peck

How Do I Love Me?
Let Me Count the Ways

Gardenias are my favorite flower and have always been my perfume of choice.

Several years ago, a client came into my office wearing the most wonderful perfume. When I asked, she shared it was "Gardenia Passion" by Annick Guttard; made in France and available only at specialty stores. I went on an immediate quest and found it at Nordstrom.

Imagine my surprise when I found a small bottle was $125. I bought it promising I would wear it only on *very* special occasions. A promise I kept until now. I read a story about a man whose wife had died unexpectedly. While cleaning out her drawers, he found a negligee she'd purchased on their trip to Paris for their honeymoon. It was still wrapped in tissue paper. She had never worn it because she was "saving it." She had not recognized how special every day is.

I realized I was doing the same thing with my Gardenia Passion. It's many years later and I am still only on my 2nd bottle. Instead of feeling special enough to wear the perfume daily, I was depriving myself and wearing another, which did not bring me the same amount of joy, my second best perfume.

I have heard if you are always enjoying the best life has to offer, you will be living your best life at every moment. Whether it is expensive French perfume, your good china or fresh flowers; you deserve the best in every moment.

Are there areas in your life where you accept less than you deserve, less than the best? What one action can you take today to show yourself how really special you are?

~ JUDI FINNERAN
Author, speaker, owner of Dharma Entities, and Co-Founder of INsight Workz, teaching unconditional self-love by example, www.dharmcoachingpath.com
www.insightworkz.com

Learning to Love Yourself CONTINUED

LOVE YOURSELF AS THY NEIGHBOR

I am a health care professional with 30 years experience. I am always perplexed and amazed how women in particular look after everybody so well. So why do they forget themselves?

Our main purpose is to look after ourselves including our physical, mental and spiritual selves. On many occasion I have had friends and strangers say you really know how to look after your self and I take it as a compliment with grace.

I pray for all women in this world to realize their most important job is to care for their physical, mental and spiritual needs. When your needs are met, you will discover you have more love, energy and desire to help as many people as you chose. You will do things—for other people from the heart, not obligation, resentment, anger or self-pity.

You say, "How do I start?" That is easy—start with the first step saying to yourself, "I love myself." Then take some action steps.

Your question is, "What action steps?" Each of us is different. Here are a few things that wok for me: time alone, walks, meditation, massage, facials, friends and family.

Just remember when you say yes to a request make sure it is really what you WANT to do. "Yes" pleases other people and "No" pleases you. Learn the art of saying "No" without feeling guilty and love yourself as thy neighbour.

~ GLORIA J. VAN DAM

Let Me Call You Sweetheart

When my high school sweetheart, Bob Walters, left and marched away with the 2nd Marine Battalion for the South Pacific in World War II, he arranged for the florist to deliver a red rose to my home with a copy of this poem by the famous Scottish poet Robert Burns. (My ancestors are Scots.)

A RED, RED ROSE

My Love is like a red, red rose
That newly blooms in June
My Love is like a melody
That's sweetly played in tune!

As fair art Thou, my bonnie lass
So deep in love am I,
And I will love thee still, my dear
'til all the seas go dry,

'Til all the seas go dry, my love
And the rocks melt with the sun
I will love thee still, my dear
While the sands of life shall run.

So fare thee well, my only Love
And fare thee well a while
And I will come again to you,
Though it be ten thousand mile.

After 4 years of each of us writing a letter every day, Bob did come back and we were married.

~ DOTTIE WALTERS, CSP
President/CEO Walters International Speakers Bureau, author of Speak and Grow Rich, *www.speakandgrowrich.com*

Let Me Call You Sweetheart continued

SWEETHEARTS FOREVER

*D*o you believe in miracles? Imagine a beautiful young blonde woman with brilliant, crystal blue eyes. She's just 15 years old. It's a sunny afternoon and she's standing on the corner waiting for a friend. Now imagine a strapping young man of 17 with hair as black as onyx and eyes as green as emeralds. He catches a quick glimpse of the girl and his heart skips a beat. This is their story.

My Mom and Dad, John and Edna Carr, were born in the early teens of the 20th century. My daddy was born in the tiny Idaho town, the 9th of 10 children and Mom was born in another small Idaho town, the 5th of 10 children. In the summer of 1931, when she was 15 years old she was visiting in Rigby, Idaho. It was there on Rigby's "bank corner" she met that strapping young man of 17, and their lives entwined forever. Three and a half months later, they eloped. Since her father had already given them an emphatic "NO" when my daddy asked his permission to marry her, it took a while for my grandfather to accept that his little girl was married. He eventually welcomed my dad into the family. Most people said it would never last.

They married during the Great Depression and started their family on a very poor farm in Idaho. Mom said there were times they weren't sure where their next meal was coming from sometimes . . . it didn't come. They raised four children and pulled together with so many others of their generation during World War II and they endured the loss of their youngest son, Neil. Their early life together was difficult on the farm, but they lived long enough to see the prosperity of the late century. For close to 70 years these lovebirds lived and loved together, demonstrating to both their children and their friends what true love was.

He was an exceptionally smart man—he loved doing any sort of math problem and was very good at "figuring things out." He was a kind and gentle man, a great father, a loving grandfather and a perfect example of a fine husband.

She was beautiful, talented and the most giving person I've ever met. She was always taking care of someone less fortunate. Her cooking abilities were legendary. How I admired and wanted to be just like her! What a wonder she was!

We kids always knew we were loved. For many years I was convinced that I was their favorite child. I was an adult before I realized they both made all of their children and 14 grandchildren feel the same way!

Mom and Dad deeply loved and cared for their family and were successfully involved in church and civic organizations. Where they truly excelled was being totally devoted to one another. The older they got, the more their lives revolved around each other. Mom and Dad harbored a true passion that they never kept secret from any of us. They had quite a reputation in their little town of being the "older couple who were always holding hands." Dad rigidly observed the rule to "kiss the cook" after every meal and in between.

I delighted in watching him kiss my Mom. My parents never passed up a chance to kiss one another or to speak loving words. It wasn't that they never had misunderstandings or downright disagreements, but they never let them get in the way for more than a few minutes. They were as necessary to one another's existence as water or air to the rest of us.

One of Dad's most important goals in his later life was to live long enough to be married to Mom for 75 years. When he told me that he had revised that to 70 years in the Spring of 2000, it gave me a jolt. I realized he had impartially evaluated his and Mom's deteriorating health. The family began to pray that they wouldn't have to be without each other for too long. They entered Hospice care on the same day.

Let Me Call You Sweetheart CONTINUED

Three days later, in the early hours, all our prayers were answered. When my brother entered their room to check on them, he found them holding hands—as always—looking so peaceful. They had passed in their sleep. In life they were never divided; and in death they were not separated.

This is what I believe happened early that Sunday morning: Dad's spirit, whole and healthy, rose above his body. He looked lovingly upon his beautiful bride of so many years. As always, he wanted her with him. He extended his hand to her and said, "Mamma, it's time to go." Without the slightest hesitation, her spirit took his hand and lovingly said, "There's no reason to stay. I'm coming, Daddy." And they walked off into the sunrise together. Even in death, they insisted on being together.

My Mom and Dad will be married for far longer than the 75 years my Dad had hoped for. You see, John and Edna will love each other for eternity because love never ends. I see proof their love every time I watch their children show affection to their spouses—every time one of their 45 grandchildren smiles— whenever one of the family gets married—whenever a new baby enters our family. These two taught all of us that love is the most precious and wonderful gift we're given. And when we cherish this gift above all else and work together to become stronger through life's obstacles, miraculous things can, and do, happen. I believe in miracles.

~ PENNY ABSHIRE
Voice actor and speaker, mother of two grown sons, married to the same wonderful guy for 36 years

TYING THE KNOT
On the Occasion of My Niece's Wedding

Whether it be seasonal or eternal, love celebrates, commemorates, but above all, it validates our need to live, because we encounter many rules and authorities in life, but none with the power to change life for the greater as love can. With love as our compass, our magnet, all else falls into place, charged and alive with passion, focus, and commitment. Let love be your teacher, guide, provider, and protector, for it is far better to put your trust in it than in the vagaries of material success.

The wedding band is simple, pure, continuous, and, as such, it is opposed to the idea of "tying the knot." Knots, we know, are convoluted, complicated, and used to hold things down. But knots also secure us with their steadfastness, so partners in marriage accept the closeness of the limits knots impose in order to preserve the purity of a lasting commitment. Thus, while love is an endless renewal of the bond, marriage itself becomes legally binding and contractual. These two forces form the heartbeat of marriage, and with love at the fore you will grow to become intimate with the joys of the wedding band, rather than the torments of a marriage bind.

So if married life seems cloudy and painful at times, take comfort in that love is like the rain which still nourishes and enriches us so that our view will clear again. This is the reason why we choose the diamond as our wedding stone. Almost all diamonds have slight occlusions and imperfections, yet they are still a marvel to behold. So take joy and pride in love, and also find strength and calmness in marriage, as we do in the stability of a rock.

~ KURT RIGHTMYER
Appeared in Maelstrom *Magazine*

Letting Go of Anger

Holding on to anger is like grasping a hot coal with the intent of throwing it at someone else; you are the one who gets burned.
~ BUDDHA

A woman is like a tea bag . . . You don't know how strong she is until you put her in hot water!
~ BUMPER STICKER

Never write a letter while you are angry.
~ CHINESE PROVERB

If a small thing has the power to make you angry, does that not indicate something about your size?
~ SYDNEY J. HARRIS

You cannot please everyone. The sooner you get this, the better off you'll be.
~ CATH KACHUR
Speaker, artist

He who angers you conquers you.
~ ELIZABETH KENNY

If you kick a stone in anger, you'll hurt your own foot.
~ KOREAN PROVERB

Resentment is like taking poison and waiting for the other person to die.
~ MALACHY MCCOURT

Letting Go of Anger CONTINUED

Hate leaves ugly scars, love leaves beautiful ones.
~ MIGNON MCLAUGHLIN

The best remedy for a short temper is a long walk.
~ JACQUELINE SCHIFF

If someone is angered or disappointed by your life, try to love that person by allowing them to be that way.
~ SANDRA SCHRIFT
Career coach, www.schrift.com

I don't have to attend every argument I'm invited to.
~ UNKNOWN

An apology is a good way to have the last word.
~ UNKNOWN

You cannot hate other people without hating your self.
~ OPRAH WINFREY

Consider to reconsider.
~ GLORIA J. VAN DAM

Letting Go of Anger CONTINUED

GIVING A BLESSING FOR AN INSULT

*T*his simple response has probably saved my marriage more than once and really helped me with angry and insulting clients, friends and relatives. It's not easy to do and it doesn't come naturally but it is really effective. When someone says something mean or insulting about you, what do you do? If you are like most people, you'll respond with an insult. Probably one that is worse than the original one. This is the start of a vicious cycle that ends up in anger, lost friendships and in some extreme cases even death. This is known as an insult for insult exchange. This is especially troubling in marriage and dating relationships. A few insulting words can lead to broken relationships and divorce. It's amazing how one angry statement can snowball into a huge confrontation.

The answer to this troubling situation is found in the Bible in 1 Peter 3:9, NLT. "Don't repay evil for evil. Don't retaliate when people say unkind things about you. Instead, pay them back with a blessing. That is what God wants you to do, and he will bless you for it." Give a blessing for an insult. This is probably one of the hardest things for a person to do, but one that can break the cycle of anger and bitterness and replace it with love and kindness. Sometimes the hurt is so great that only God can help us with the blessing. The next time you find yourself in an escalating confrontation, take a step back, take a breath and give a blessing for an insult. You'll be amazed at the results!

~ JOHN RICHARDSON
Speaker, www.SuccessBeginsToday.com

Life

The rules of a happy life are these: Smile, Have Fun, and Be Wild and Crazy. Risk ridicule and enjoy the moment.

~ CYNTHIA BRIAN
Speaker, author of the New York Times *best-selling* Chicken Soup for the Gardener's Soul, Be the Star You Are!, The Business of Show Business *and others. www.star-style.com*

I don't want life to imitate art. I want life to be art.

~ CARRIE FISHER

Bring love into this day. This moment is all we have, and all we will ever have, and it is where we find the joy and power of God's presence.

~ MARY MANIN MORRISSEY
Author of Life Keys

You are more than your physical body—you are an energetic being.

~ CAROLINE MYSS

While we have the gift of life, it seems to me the only tragedy is to allow part of us to die whether it is our spirit, our creativity or our glorious uniqueness.

~ GILDA RADNER

If I were a caterpillar I would like to hang out on a wall where little children gather to talk about life and love so that I would be able to have colorful words of wisdom to take with me on my upcoming journey.

~ CATHERINE TILLEY
Founder of the Institute for Global Healing and Publisher of WISE Publications www.theglobalvoice.com

Life is not measured by the number of breaths we take but by the moments that take our breath away.

~ UNKNOWN

Life

KID'S RULES FOR LIFE

Never trust a dog to watch your food.
~ PATRICK, AGE 10

When you want something expensive, ask your grandparents.
~ MATTHEW, AGE 12

Wear a hat when feeding seagulls.
~ ROCKY, AGE 9

Never try to hide a piece of broccoli in a glass of milk.
~ ROSEMARY, AGE 7

Never bug a pregnant mom.
~ NICHOLAS, AGE 11

Don't ever be too full for dessert.
~ KELLY, AGE 10

When your dad is mad and asks you, "Do I look stupid?" don't answer
him.
~ HEATHER, AGE 16

Never tell your mom her diet's not working.
~ MICHAEL, AGE 14

When you get a bad grade in school, show it to mom when she's on
the phone.
~ ALYESHA, AGE 13

Life CONTINUED

Never try to baptize a cat.
~ LAURA, AGE 13

Beware of cafeteria food when it looks like it's moving.
~ ROB, AGE 10

Never tell your little brother that you're not going to do
what your mom told you to do.
~ HANK, AGE 12

Never dare your little brother to paint the family car.
~ PHILLIP, AGE 13

45 RULES OF LIFE

1. Give people more than they expect and do it cheerfully.
2. Memorize your favorite poem.
3. Don't believe all you hear, spend all you have or sleep all you want.
4. When you say, "I love you", mean it.
5. When you say, "I'm sorry", look the person in the eye.
6. Be engaged at least six months before you get married.
7. Believe in love at first sight.
8. Never laugh at anyone's dreams.
9. Love deeply and passionately. You might get hurt but it's the only way to live life completely.
10. In disagreements, fight fairly. No name calling.

Life CONTINUED

11. Don't judge people by their relatives.

12. Talk slow but think quick.

13. When someone asks you a question you don't want to answer, smile and ask, "Why do you want to know?"

14. Remember that great love and great achievements involve great risk.

15. Call your mom.

16. Say "bless you" when you hear someone sneeze.

17. When you lose, don't lose the lesson.

18. Remember the three R's: Respect for self; Respect for others; Responsibility for all your actions.

19. Don't let a little dispute injure a great friendship.

20. When you realize you've made a mistake, take immediate steps to correct it.

21. Smile when picking up the phone. The caller will hear it in your voice.

22. Marry a man you love to talk to. As you get older, his conversational skills will be as important as any other.

23. Spend some time alone.

24. Open your arms to change, but don't let go of your values.

25. Remember that silence is sometimes the best answer.

26. Read more books and watch less TV.

27. Live a good, honorable life. Then when you get older and think back, you'll get to enjoy it a second time.

28. Trust in God but lock your car.

29. A loving atmosphere in your home is so important. Do all you can to create a tranquil harmonious home.

30. In disagreements with loved ones, deal with the current situation. Don't bring up the past.

31. Read between the lines.

32. Share your knowledge. It's a way to achieve immortality.

33. Be gentle with the earth.

34. Pray. There's immeasurable power in it.

35. Never interrupt when you are being flattered.

36. Mind your own business.

37. Don't trust a man who doesn't close his eyes when you kiss him.

38. Once a year, go someplace you've never been before.

39. If you make a lot of money, put it to use helping others while you are living. That is wealth's greatest satisfaction.

40. Remember that not getting what you want is sometimes a stroke of luck.

41. Learn the rules, then break some.

42. Remember that the best relationship is one where your love for each other is greater than your need for each other.

43. Judge your success by what you had to give up in order to get it.

44. Remember that your character is your destiny.

45. Approach love and cooking with reckless abandon.

~ UNKNOWN

Living with Joy

I thought I was pretty hot stuff. I was 23 years old and had landed a job as a paralegal in a high-powered law firm. I had my own office, wore suits and got to carry a briefcase. I had arrived. My first day on the job I was introduced around to the secretaries and lawyers. As I was getting set up in my office feeling important, I heard a voice behind me. I turned around and there standing at the door was a middle-aged woman dressed in horrid polyester stretch pants and a shirt, obviously purchased at KMart, hanging over her pants and hiding her somewhat ample belly. She extended her hand and introduced herself as Bev, the file clerk. I shook her hand. Her grip was strong. She had cropped gray hair and dark almost black eyes that crinkled up in the corners when she smiled at me. Her voice was deep and melodious with just a hint of a southern accent. She told me if there was anything I needed to be sure and let her know. She was by far the friendliest person I met in this austere and stiff law firm.

As the days turned into weeks and the weeks into months, I grew more and more disillusioned with the job. Frankly, it was hopelessly boring indexing a plethora of documents all day and summarizing depositions of long-winded attorneys. I was miserable. I found myself frequently going into Bev's little room. It was more like a closet with no windows and piles of Bekins boxes. Somehow, amidst the beautiful corner offices overlooking the bay, I sought refuge in this little closet. I found myself revealing my soul and innermost thoughts to this woman who put whatever work aside she was doing and listened with no judgment, with interest and with her heart. My spirits were always lifted when I left her room. I didn't realize it at the time, but she made me feel like someone cared and loved me. I had never felt that way.

She had poor health and was in the hospital several times with bleeding ulcers. But every time I went to see her, she downplayed her pain and insisted on talking about what was going on in my life. She never dwelled on her pain and didn't want to discuss it even when she developed an incredibly painful mouth cancer.

My life went in a different direction, but we still met for lunch on occasion. I called her one day and her husband sadly informed me that she was dying of cancer and wasn't expected to live beyond the next day. I wept when I got off of the phone for this incredible woman who treated the senior partner the same as the homeless man on the street, who knew the names of everyone's kids and spouses and always asked about them, who talked to people in the elevator and who even melted the heart of the most hard-bitten attorney in the firm.

I realize now what a rare and precious woman she was. She is the only person I have ever met who always lived in a loving and nurturing space, who never judged and had really mastered the art of listening. She taught me much about not judging, listening and loving. I have worn polyester and have shopped at KMart and have been blessed with the gift of Bev's friendship and love.

~ TERRY SWEENEY

Living with Joy CONTINUED

To This Day

*A*t 17 years old I was a student nurse in the nursery; this was the mid-60s—when nurses were mean to their younger co-workers. I was told to take a dead 3-day-old baby to the morgue that was seven floors below the nursery. On my way down as I held this dead baby in my arms, a major epiphany occurred. What came to me: Life was short and I need to make the most of each day. As a result of that event, I have lived my life to the utmost.

To this day I have only one regret—that I didn't see Elvis Presley do a live show.

Many people question why do babies or young children die. My take is they die to teach us lessons and my lesson changed my life dramatically as well as other people who are part of my life.

To this day, I will never forget the event; I thank the baby for only one regret in my life.

To this day in my life this was the most dramatic and memorable event in my whole life!

~ GLORIA J. VAN DAM

Love

Love is patient, love is kind. It does not envy, it does not boast, it is not proud. It is not rude, it is not self-seeking, it is not easily angered, it keeps no record of wrongs. Love does not delight in evil but rejoices with the truth. It always protects, always trusts, always perseveres. Love never fails. But where there are prophecies, they will cease; where there are tongues, they will be stilled; where there is knowledge, it will pass away . . . And now these things remain: faith, hope and love. But the greatest of these is love.

~ 1 CORINTHIANS 13:1–8, 13

Everyone admits that love is wonderful and necessary, yet no one can agree on what it is.

~ DIANE ACKERMAN

Love is that condition in the human spirit so profound that it allows me to survive, and better than that, to thrive with passion, compassion, and style.

~ MAYA ANGELOU
American poet, writer, and actress

Love. What is love? No word can define it, it's something so great, only God could design it. Yes, love is beyond, what man can define, for love is immortal, and God's gift is Divine.

~ ANONYMOUS

Love is, above all, the gift of oneself.

~ JEAN ANOUILH

Love continued

First learn to love and accept yourself unconditionally. Then you can truly love and accept someone else.
~ PATRICE BAKER
Speaker, author, www.PowerOfWords.com

Loving ourselves and others is what a good life is all about.
~ LYDIA BOYD

It's love if they order one of those desserts that are on fire. They like to order those because it's just like how their hearts are—on fire.
~ CHRISTINE, AGE 9, *KID'S THEOLOGY*

Whatever our souls are made of, his and mine are the same.
~ EMILY BRONTË

I love you not only for what you are, but for what I am when I am with you. I love you not only for what you have made of yourself, but for what you are making of me. I love you for the part of me that you bring out.
~ ELIZABETH BARRETT BROWNING
English poet, Feminist 1806–1861

You yourself, as much as anybody in the entire universe, deserve your love and affection.
~ BUDDHA

The expression of love is often demonstrated in a variety of forms, some of which may not be obvious.
~ BETTY COLSTON

Love

You never lose by loving. You always lose by holding back.

~ BARBARA DE ANGELIS
Speaker, author

Love is what light feels like.

~ DAVID DEIDA

Love is always the perfect gift.

~ DOVE MILK CHOCOLATE WRAPPER
Submitted by Barbara C. Lemaire, PhD, Inspired Collaboration

It makes one warm to feel love but makes one glow to be loved.

~ BECKY FARTASH

Nobody has ever measured, even poets, how much a heart can hold.

~ ZELDA FITZGERALD

You learn to speak by speaking, to study by studying, to run by running, to work by working; in just the same way, you learn to love by loving.

~ ANATOLE FRANCE
French writer, Nobel Prizes for Literature

Anyone can be passionate, but it takes real lovers to be silly.

~ ROSE FRANKEN

Love makes time pass; time makes love pass.

~ FRENCH PROVERB

Love CONTINUED

Love is a game that two can play and both win.
~ EVA GABOR

If I had a single flower for every time I think about you, I could walk forever in my garden.
~ CLAUDIA GHANDI

Where there is love there is life.
~ INDIRA GANDHI
Indian Prime Minister

The heart that loves is always young.
~ GREEK PROVERB

Love is the great miracle cure. Loving ourselves works miracles in our lives.
~ LOUISE L. HAY, SPEAKER
Author of You Can Heal Your Life

Love is the great miracle cure. Loving ourselves works miracles in our lives.
~ LOUISE L. HAY, SPEAKER
Author of You Can Heal Your Life

The truth is that there is only one terminal dignity—love. And the story of a love is not important—what is important is that one is capable of love. It is perhaps the only glimpse we are permitted of eternity.
~ HELEN HAYES

Love CONTINUED

We do not fall in love with the package of the person,
we fall in love with the inside of a person.

~ ANNE HECHE

Thru mysterious means, love travels . . . into closed hearts and opens
them. Eventually.

~ CATH KACHUR
Speaker, artist, www.HumanTuneUp.com

Never let a problem to be solved become more important than the
person to be loved.

~ BARBARA JOHNSON
Best-selling writer

Love is everything it's cracked up to be. That's why people are so cyn-
ical about it. It really is worth fighting for, being brave for, risking
everything for. And the trouble is, if you don't risk anything, you risk
even more.

~ ERICA JONG
Writer, feminist

There's exciting love and humdrum love. It's all love.

~ CATH KACHUR
Speaker, author of artist, www.humanTuneUp.com

Love is always present, it is just a matter of feeling it or not.

~ KIMBERLY KIRBERG

Love CONTINUED

Love is missing someone whenever you're apart, but somehow feeling warm inside because you're close in heart.

~ KAY KNUDSEN

Love is like the sun: has its inner energy source that shines on you.

~ HELENE LAGERBERG

Love is a verb.

~ CLARE BOOTHE LUCE
Playwright, diplomat

I love the way you smile at me, I love the way your hands reach out and hold me near. . . . I believe this is heaven to no one else but me.

~ SARAH MCLACHLAN

We choose those we like; with those we love, we have no say in the matter.

~ MIGNON MCLAUGHLIN

Start living now. Stop saving the good china for that special occasion. Stop withholding your love until that special person materializes. Every day you are alive is a special occasion. Every minute, every breath, is a gift from God.

~ MARY MANIN MORRISSEY
Author of Life Keys

I have one thing that counts, and that is my heart; it burns in my soul, it aches in my flesh, and it ignites my nerves: that is my love for the people and Peron.

~ EVITA PERON
Argentinian President, 1919–1952

Love CONTINUED

When two people love each other, they don't look at each other, they look in the same direction.

~ GINGER ROGERS

Before I met my husband, I'd never fallen in love.
I'd stepped in it a few times.

~ RITA RUDNER

Your task is not to seek for love, but merely to seek
and find all the barriers within yourself that you have built against it.

~ DJALAL AD-DIN RUMI
Persian mystic and poet, 1207–1273

How can you tell if two adults eating dinner at a restaurant are in love?
Romantic adults usually are all dressed up, so if they are just wearing
jeans it might mean they used to go out or they just broke up.

~ SARAH, AGE 9, *KID'S THEOLOGY*

Love is more than a feeling. It is a conscious and consistent choice.
When you give love you get love.

~ SANDRA SCHRIFT
Career coach, www.schrift.com

Love is a force that connects us to every strand of the universe, an
unconditional state that characterizes human nature, a form of knowledge that is always there for us if only we can open ourselves to it.

~ EMILY HILBURN SELL

In real love you want the other person's good. In romantic love, you
want the other person.

~ MARGARET CHASE SMITH

Love CONTINUED

There is nothing more important in life than love.
~ BARBRA STREISAND

To be kind to all, to like many and love a few, to be needed and wanted by those we love, is certainly the nearest we can come to happiness.
~ MARY STUART

Give God full permission.
~ MOTHER TERESA

There are four questions of value in life . . . What is sacred? Of what is the spirit made? What is worth living for, and what is worth dying for? The answer to each is the same. Only love.
~ UNKNOWN

For an instant, love can transform the world.
~ UNKNOWN

Love—a wildly misunderstood although highly desirable malfunction of the heart which weakens the brain, causes eyes to sparkle, cheeks to glow, blood pressure to rise and the lips to pucker.
~ UNKNOWN

Love would never be a promise of a rose garden unless it is showered with light of faith, water of sincerity and air of passion.
~ UNKNOWN

Just because somebody doesn't love you the way you want them to, doesn't mean they don't love you with all they have.
~ UNKNOWN

Love CONTINUED

You learn to like someone when you find out what makes them laugh, but you can never truly love someone until you find out what makes them cry.

~ UNKNOWN

Sometimes we make love with our eyes.
Sometimes we make love with our hands.
Sometimes we make love with our bodies.
Always we make love with our hearts.

~ UNKNOWN

Love is to let those we love be perfectly themselves, and not to twist them to fit our own image . . . otherwise we love only the reflection of ourselves we find in them.

~ UNKNOWN

Love isn't finding a perfect person. It's seeing an imperfect person perfectly.

~ UNKNOWN

The spiritual meaning of love is measured by what it can do. Love is meant to heal. Love is meant to renew. Love is meant to bring us closer to God.

~ UNKNOWN

If you give your life as a wholehearted response to love, then love will wholeheartedly respond to you. Love is the intuitive knowledge of our hearts.

~ MARIANNE WILLIAMSON
Author of A Return to Love

Love CONTINUED

Miracles occur naturally as expressions of love. The real miracle is the love that inspires them. In this sense everything that comes from love is miracle.

~ MARIANNE WILLIAMSON
Author of A Return to Love

LOVE IS LIKE . . . .

. . . a rollercoaster; when you first get on, you're scared and all these emotions occur. When you let go and put your hands in the air, you feel something real and happy.

~ CAITLIN

. . . the wind . . . You can't see it, but you can feel it.

~ FROM THE MOVIE *A WALK TO REMEMBER*

. . . oxygen. Love is a many-splendored thing.

~ FROM THE MOVIE *MOULIN ROUGE*

. . . a river, never ending as it flows, but gets greater with time!

~ UNKNOWN

. . . a fire that reigns in the heart.

~ UNKNOWN

THIS LOVE

This love.
This space.
This minuscule of time we share
is sheltered in our hearts.
Cherished fleeting memories
seek chambers in which to rest.
When the clock strikes
and the chimes of time slow
or ring no more,
each shining moment will rise
and fill the empty space
with joy
and laughter
and music . . .
and we will dance
our finest dance,
and touch
and feel
and love, my dear,
once more.

~ MARY LENORE QUIGLEY
Author of By Fools Like Me: Heart Songs in Verse

Love CONTINUED

LOVE IS A CHOICE

love is pure outpouring
as a river's natural flow
gentle as the flakes falling
in Winter's first snow

it is the anticipation felt
as a rose begins to bloom
we ask, what will love unfold?
will it bring joy or gloom?

it is as innocent as a baby
crying out in the night
dependent wholly on another
to be guided toward the light

love is fierce
like a fire uncontained
as forceful as
the thundering rain
        demanding, sometimes
causing pain

        and when love is not returned in kind
can adversely affect the mind of those
who depend upon its light
to help them make it through the night

upon the rise of each new sun
love is revived anew and so
it is available to me and you

love is a choice
I'm trying to say
that never, ever goes away

~ PATRICE C. BAKER
Speaker, life coach author of The Power of Words: Poetry and Prose for Powerful Living
www.ThePowerOfWords.com

LOVE IS THE REWARD OF LOVE

When I was young, my mom said something that terrified me. She loved her children so much, she said, that she'd cut off her right arm to save our lives. I had nightmares that she might actually have to do it—how could she hug us?

It wasn't until I became a parent myself that I recognized the reality of such unconditional love. Mom sacrificed selflessly to give her children great food, a great education, and great self-esteem and self-worth. Mom was involved in all our activities. She attended all our sports, cheerleading, 4-H events, volunteering for every parent committee so she would stay involved with her children.

At Christmas, Dad would take us kids shopping, and we'd each buy Mom our favorite present. (Every Christmas, Mom got five flannel Mother Hubbard nightgowns!) For her birthdays, we showered her with homemade gifts such as cookies, colored leaves, knitted items, and hand-framed photos. We cooked her a special dinner, and Dad always made a big to-do about his "Queen." We treasured her dearly within the family, but we'd never celebrated her publicly.

Love CONTINUED

When her 70th birthday approached, my two sisters, my brother, and I decided it was time to give Mom a big surprise party to show our appreciation for all those years. Keeping it a surprise turned out to be a considerable feat. We booked a rural firehouse transforming it into a Garden of Eden. All her children, grandchildren, and spouses came to help set up. Trellises, birdhouses, hoses, water buckets, garden tools, rakes, potted plants, candles, potpourri, garden lights, hummingbird feeders, and all types of beautiful accessories adorned the tables and walls, while hundreds of balloons in wine colors floated through the air. Then the guests started to arrive, hundreds of them, laden with more gardening gifts and bringing their wonderful stories of Mom.

Mom arrived to a fireworks and rocket display, thanks to her grandson Justin, and was totally surprised. The love that filled that firehouse could have ignited a real fire. To have reached the age of 70 and to have so many true friends and loving relatives celebrating her life was indescribably wonderful. As people danced, ate, and laughed, I realized that the only thing in life that truly endures is love. As Goethe said, "Love is the reward of love."

~ CYNTHIA BRIAN
Speaker, author of the New York Times *best-selling* Chicken Soup for the Gardener's Soul, Be the Star You Are!, The Business of Show Business *and others. www.star-style.com*

Love Lost

It's a long road when you face the world alone,
when no one reaches out a hand for you to hold.
You can find love if you search within your soul,
and the emptiness you felt will disappear.

~ MARIAH CAREY
Singer, song lyrics

Don't make my mistake. Don't let yourself be so angry that you stop loving. Because one day you'll wake up from that anger, and the person you love will be gone.

~ FROM THE TV SERIES *DAWSON'S CREEK*

The bad things in life open your eyes to the good things you weren't paying attention to before.

~ FROM THE MOVIE *GOOD WILL HUNTING*

Whatever place we complete a relationship is the place where we begin the next. Complete with loving closure.

~ SHERYL ROUSH
Speaker, author of Sparkle-Tudes! *and* Heart of A Mother, *www.SparklePresentations.com*

I know what it does to you, I know. Maybe that's why we hold on as hard as we do. We just can't believe that such a miracle can happen to us twice. But it can, someday you'll find it again.

~ FROM THE MOVIE *SOMEONE LIKE YOU*

I can remember so very well the day that he toppled off that white horse— but it took me years to realize that it was really I who was knocked off that horse by my high expectations and misperceptions of love.

~ CATHERINE TILLEY
Founder of the Institute for Global Healing and Publisher of WISE Publications
www.theglobalvoice.com

Love Lost continued

The best way to lose love is to hold it tightly.
~ UNKNOWN

Some people think that it's holding on that makes one strong; sometimes it's letting go.
~ UNKNOWN

You will know that you love someone when you want him/her to be happy. Even if that means you're not a part of their happiness.
~ UNKNOWN

The heart does heal and you will love like this again . . . only when you do, you will deny you ever felt like this before.
~ UNKNOWN

Don't cry because it's over, smile because it happened.
~ UNKNOWN

Why am I afraid to lose you when you're not even mine . . .
~ UNKNOWN

BITTERSWEET
You are like a deep breath of pleasure.
You exist real and warm in my life.
You bring waves of feelings
And happy smiles.
I am glad

THEN YOU ARE GONE

As if you were a dream or a thought . . .
BITTERSWEET.

You are fine.
You are so considerate and sharing.
So much, here for me, near to me.
I am glad.

THEN YOU ARE GONE

There remains a comfort to think
That maybe you will near to me . . . again.
BITTERSWEET

You are warm.
I love to rise to your touch
I reach for the lovely burn of your hands.
To cuddle in their care.
I am glad

THEN YOU ARE GONE.

The heat from my body and
From my legs reflect
Cool nothingness and
Ache with a memory.
BITTERSWEET

~ CASSANDRA NORTHINGTON

Making a Difference

The area where we are the greatest is the area in which we inspire, encourage, and connect with another human being.

~ MAYA ANGELOU
American poet, writer, and actress

When you tell someone that who they are makes a difference—they do!

~ HELICE "THE SPARK" BRIDGES
Author of Who I Am Makes A Difference, *Founder and President of Difference Makers International*

A good deed on an unpleasant day shines forth and lights up the disguised blessings.

~ BETTY COLSTON

God loves a cheerful giver.

~ II CORINTHIANS 9:7

Everyone needs to be valued. Everyone has the potential to give something back.

~ DIANA, PRINCESS OF WALES

Extend love. Help the world work.

~ CATH KACHUR, SPEAKER, AUTHOR OF ARTIST

Making a Difference

Enthusiasm is at the heart of any positive change in the world. Each of us have something to offer to uplift the spirit of others, whether through achieving a lifelong goal that inspires children to make better choices, influencing friends to a healthier way of life, helping people heal themselves, creating a joyful workplace or home, or connecting more deeply with family, nature, or a cause. In all of its expressions, enthusiasm is a gift to be shared with the world. Enthusiasm, however you define it, is at the core of all success. Whether you're hoping to achieve a big dream, heal your body, find peace of mind, influence a client to choose your product, push for a promotion, derive more pleasure from your community or church, or have deeper committed relationships with those you love, enthusiasm can help.

~ MARY MARCDANTE
Speaker, author of Living with Enthusiasm
www.MaryMarcdante.com

Never doubt that a small group of thoughtful, committed citizens can change the world. Indeed, it's the only thing that ever has.

~ MARGARET MEAD

We can do no great things, only small things with great love.

~ MOTHER TERESA

Begin doing what you want to do now WE are not living in eternity. We have only his moment, sparkling like a star in our hand—and melting like a snowflake.

~ MARIE REYNON RAY

Making a Difference CONTINUED

In politics, if you want anything said, ask a man; if you want anything done, ask a woman.

~ MARGARET THATCHER

Our inner strengths, experiences, and truths cannot be lost, destroyed, or taken away. Every person has an inborn worth and can contribute to the human community. We all can treat one another with dignity and respect, provide opportunities to grow toward our fullest lives and help one another discover and develop our unique gifts. We each deserve this and we all can extend it to others.

~ UNKNOWN

The true stewardship of a woman lies not in what she has, but in how she affects the lives of others.

~ RHEBA WASHINGTON-LINDSEY
Author of Teaching Isn't For Cowards

With every deed you are sowing a seed, though the harvest you may not see.

~ ELLA WHEELER WILCOX

In every community, there is work to be done.
In every nation, there are wounds to heal.
In every heart, there is the power to do it.

~ MARIANNE WILLIAMSON
Author of A Woman's Worth

Devote today to something so daring even you can't believe you're doing it.

~ OPRAH WINFREY

Marriage

*W*hen I was getting married many years ago, a man I worked with gave me this advice. He said God had some really good simple plans. God intended marriage to be between two people, and the two people only. When two people get married he is not marrying her family and she is not marrying his family. Over the years you will find that troubles usually come from the intervention of an external source—in-laws, finances, etc. When dealing with issues, the two people should stick together, recognize the external intervention, keep it external to their marriage and not allow the external pressures to divide them. If things get really out of hand, the couple may need to ask themselves "If this problem were to go away, would our relationship still be good?" If the answer is yes, then the marriage is solid. If the answer is no, you may need to dig a little deeper. In simple terms if you did not have a huge mortgage payment and bills, would your life be wonderful? If this is the case, then work the issue together, knowing you have something precious and worth hanging on to. Now I have used his advice many times over the last 30 years and I must declare, I never thought marriage could be this good!

~ JUDY TEJWANI

Marriage CONTINUED

INGREDIENTS FOR A HAPPY MARRIAGE

1. Mutual respect.
2. Care for each other at all times.
3. Enjoy being together. It probably helps to have mutual interests.
4. Talking together for hours at a time.
5. Understanding—more great talking.
6. Being supportive of each other, in every way.
7. Great pride and loyalty to each other.
8. Settle a disagreement immediately.

Although we were married with no pre-conceived ideas about love and marriage, we seemed to think alike, and were engaged in two weeks after we met on May 30, 1947. The items mentioned above are the result of our love, and we have had 57 years of a very happy marriage. I still think my husband Jim is the finest, and most wonderful man in the world, a great husband, father (4), and grandfather (10) to our large family.

~ JULIA ROUSH

TAPESTRY PERSONIFIED

If I wove a tapestry
Of the times we've shared
There would be colors so rich
Yet, threads that are bare.

Tapestry scenes would
Show dreams yet fulfilled
Young passionate hearts
In the hunt of the thrill

In the shadow are hurts
Woven in by the loom
Scenes in the background
Depicted in gloom

Rekindled feelings
Are envisioned beyond
Interlaced with passion
Never really quite gone

Similarities are muted
In hues much the same
Incongruity diverges
Then comes back again

Commitment runs through
The one constant thread
Brightest in color pattern
Even bolder than red

If I wove a tapestry
Of the times we've shared
There would be colors so rich
Yet, threads that are bare
But, none would compare
No—none would compare

~ LEE A. BARRON
Publisher, author
© Copyright 2000 Lee A. Barron

Marriage CONTINUED

A man without a wife is like a vase without flowers.

~ AFRICAN PROVERB

Love: A temporary insanity curable by marriage.

~ AMBROSE BIERCE
Journalist

It is only possible to live happily ever after on a day-to-day basis.

~ MARGARET BONNANO

A good marriage is one which allows for change and growth
in the individuals and in the way they express their love.

~ PEARL S. BUCK
Author of Nobel Prize for Literature, 1938

I never knew what happiness was until I got married . . . .
And then it was too late!

~ SUSAN CLARKE, SPEAKER, AUTHOR

For two people in a marriage to live together day after day
is unquestionably the one miracle the Vatican has overlooked.

~ BILL COSBY
Author of Love and Marriage

Never go to bed mad. Stay up and fight.

~ PHYLLIS DILLER
Author of Phyllis Diller's Housekeeping Hints

Marriage CONTINUED

The kind of marriage you make depends upon the kind of person you are. If you are a happy, well-adjusted person, the chances are your marriage will be a happy one. If you have made adjustments so far with more satisfaction than distress, you are likely to make your marriage and family adjustments satisfactorily. If you are discontented and bitter about your lot in life, you will have to change before you can expect to live happily ever after.

~ EVELYN DUVALL
Author of When You Marry

A man in love is incomplete until he has married. Then he's finished.

~ ZSA ZSA GABOR

A happy marriage is the union of two good forgivers.

~ RUTH BELL GRAHAM

When you realize you want to spend the rest of your life with somebody, you want the rest of your life to start as soon as possible.

~ FROM THE MOVIE WHEN *HARRY MET SALLY*

Sometimes I wonder if men and women really suit each other. Perhaps they should live next door and just visit now and then.

~ KATHARINE HEPBURN

I have learned that only two things are necessary to keep one's wife happy. First, let her think she's having her own way. And second, let her have it.

~ LYNDON B. JOHNSON
Former President of the United States

Marriage CONTINUED

Marrying a man is like buying something you've been admiring for a long time in a shop window. You may love it when you get it home, but it doesn't always go with everything in the house.

~ JEAN KERR

A successful marriage requires falling in love many times, always with the same person.

~ MIGNON MCLAUGHLIN

Successful marriage is always a triangle: a man, a woman, and God.

~ CECIL MYERS

In the 1970s my friends brothers' wife who is an astrologer, read my chart. When it came to love and romance she said I would marry late and marry well. I was in my early 20s at a that time. Here's the late where's the "well???"

~ BECKY PALMER
Age 52, never married

When Dolly Parton was asked by Melissa Etheridge on *Oprah*, "Do you believe in same-sex marriages?" Dolly replied, "Hell yes! Why shouldn't you folks have the same tough times we go through!"

I think men who have a pierced ear are better prepared for marriage. They've experienced pain and bought jewelry.

~ RITA RUDNER

I love being married. It's so great to find that one special person you want to annoy for the rest of your life.

~ RITA RUDNER

Marriage

In the opinion of the world, marriage ends all, as it does in a comedy. The truth is precisely the opposite: it begins all.

~ ANNE SOPHIE SWETCHINE

Don't fight over anything that won't matter a year from now. Where you have dinner tonight does not matter in the big picture. Having dinner together (functioning as a couple) does matter.

~ JUDY TEJWANI

Spouse: someone who'll stand by you through all the trouble you wouldn't have had if you'd stayed single.

~ UNKNOWN

Marriage means commitment. Of course, so does insanity.

~ UNKNOWN

Adam and Eve had an ideal marriage. He didn't have to hear about all the men she could have married, and she didn't have to hear about the way his mother cooked.

~ UNKNOWN

One advantage of marriage it seems to me—
Is that when you fall out of love with him
Or he falls out of love with you
It keeps you together until maybe you fall in again.

~ JUDITH VIORST

Marriage is a great institution, but I'm not ready for an institution.

~ MAE WEST

Marriage CONTINUED

FIVE MAGIC WORDS

*B*efore the age of 35 I was a dysfunctional relationship magnet and a crazed workaholic with a staff instead of kids, a beautiful office instead of a home, and a big thick daybook instead of a life. Suddenly I found myself numb from the waist down, partially blind and diagnosed with multiple sclerosis.

I was *blocked*. To heal from MS, I had to bust my way out of thoughts and emotions that were killing me. I also had to find love for someone I didn't even know—myself. One promise I made was to never have another broken heart, thus I swore off men, forever—or so I thought.

Enter my soulmate. Before healing from MS, the man of my dreams would have had nothing to do with the cigarette smoking, junk-food junkie, workaholic woman that I had been. When I stopped the charade of my life and started looking for the real me, I cleared the path for Jack, a man who reflected the values for which I was searching. He was willing to sift through all the outside facades I was so attached to in order to get to the inner core of who I was. He saw the star under the rock and helped me see it, too. He helped me get there, and by so doing, he got to the inner core of himself.

We have now been married for 17 wonderful years. That's not to say we don't have disagreements. But we have five magic words that keep us together. I'll never forget the night I discovered those magic words. "I have it!" I shrieked. "I have the secret to our loving relationship. We've said it to each other a million times. Over and over we both take deep breaths, look past all the nonsense and straight into each other's hearts. Over and over we utter the same five words . . . "

Jack smiled his great smile and looked deep into my eyes as we said together, "But I love you anyway."

~ JUDITH PARKER HARRIS, SPEAKER
Author of Master Challenges in Your Life and Move From Blocked to Block-Buster
www.healthesteem.com

Men!

Ever notice how all of women's problems start with men? MENtal illness, MENstrual cramps, MENtal breakdown, MENopause. And when we have real problems, it's HIS-terectomy! Don't forget the "GUY"-necologist!

~ ANONYMOUS

WHAT WOMEN SAY ABOUT MEN...

Men can read maps better than women. 'Cause only the male mind could conceive of one inch equaling a hundred miles.

~ ROSEANNE BARR

What's with you men? Would hair stop growing on your chest if you asked directions somewhere?

~ ERMA BOMBECK

If the world were a logical place, men would ride side-saddle.

~ RITA MAE BROWN

Part of the reason that men seem so much less loving than women is that men's behavior is measured with a feminine ruler.

~ FRANCESCA M. CANCIAN

You don't develop courage by being happy in your relationships everyday. You develop it by surviving difficult times and challenging adversity.

~ BARBARA DE ANGELIS

If men can run the world, why can't they stop wearing neckties? How intelligent is it to start the day by tying a little noose around your neck?

~ LINDA ELLERBEE

Men! CONTINUED

Men were made for war. Without it they wandered greyly about, getting under the feet of the women, who were trying to organize the really important things of life.
~ ALICE THOMAS ELLIS

God made man stronger but not necessarily more intelligent. He gave women intuition and femininity. And, used properly, that combination easily jumbles the brain of any man I've ever met.
~ FARRAH FAWCETT

My theory is that men are no more liberated than women.
~ INDIRA GANDHI

A man's got to do what a man's got to do. A woman must do what he can't.
~ RHONDA HANSOME

The test of man is how well he is able to feel about what he thinks. The test of a woman is how well she is able to think about what she feels.
~ MARY MCDOWELL

I wonder why men get serious at all. They have this delicate, long thing hanging outside their bodies which goes up and down by its own will. If I were a man I would always be laughing at myself.
~ YOKO ONO

Can you imagine a world without men? No crime and lots of happy fat women.
~ MARION SMITH AND NICOLE HOLLANDER

Men!

The smell of a woman should stay with you. The smell of a man should come to you as you go to him and leave you with only a memory, not a headache.

~ DANIELLE STEELE

I know I am truly loved. I know this because whenever a situation arises where the man I adore must make a choice between my needs and his own he consistently and without hesitation, chooses to honor me rather than merely satisfying above his own immediate needs and desires.

~ CATHERINE TILLEY
Founder of the Institute for Global Healing and Publisher of WISE Publications
www.theglobalvoice.com

A successful man is one who makes more money than his wife can spend. A successful woman is one who can find such a man.

~ LANA TURNER

When a man talks dirty to a woman, it's sexual harassment. When a woman talks dirty to a man, it's $3.95 a minute.

~ UNKNOWN

The only difference between men and boys is the cost of their toys.

~ UNKNOWN

You [men] are not our protectors . . . If you were, who would there be to protect us from?

~ MARY EDWARDS WALKER

Give a man a free hand and he'll run it all over you.

~ MAE WEST

Men! CONTINUED

A man can be short and dumpy and getting bald but if he has fire, women will like him.
~ MAE WEST

A man over time falls in love with the woman he is attracted to, and a woman over time becomes more attracted to the man she loves.
~ JENNIFER WILKINSON

A lot of guys think the larger a woman's breasts are, the less intelligent she is. I don't think it works like that. I think it's the opposite. I think the larger a woman's breasts are, the less intelligent the men become.
~ ANITA WISE

WHAT MEN SAY ABOUT WOMEN ...

When you can see your unborn children in her arms, you know you really love a woman.
~ BRYAN ADAMS

To get to a woman's heart, a man must first use his own.
~ MIKE DOBBERTIN
Quoted in A Fifth Portion of Chicken Soup for the Soul

There is in every true woman's heart a spark of heavenly fire, which lies dormant in the broad daylight of prosperity; but which kindles up, and beams and blazes in the dark hour of adversity.
~ WASHINGTON IRVING

Men! CONTINUED

Every woman needs one man in her life who is strong and responsible. Given this security, she can proceed to do what she really wants to do—fall in love with men who are weak and irresponsible.

~ RICHARD J. NEEDHAM

Real love is when you become selfless and you are more concerned about your mate's or children's egos than your own. You're now a giver instead of a taker.

~ SYLVESTER STALLONE
Actor, best known as the character "Rocky"

Men always want to be a woman's first love—women like to be a mans last romance.

~ OSCAR WILDE, IRISH POET

God gave us all a penis and a brain, but only enough blood to run one at a time.

~ ROBIN WILLIAMS, COMEDIAN

On the one hand, we'll never experience childbirth. On the other hand, we can open all our own jars.

~ BRUCE WILLIS
On the difference between men and women

Men never remember, but women never forget.

~ UNKNOWN

IN MY BEAUTIFUL DREAM
Written while courting for Choon Mah-Meggett

My desire for you is like a fragile soap bubble . . .
tenuously floating on the gentle breath of the wind
then lighting on the sleeping face of God.

Holding on while still savoring the moment . . .
knowing this special moment won't last for long.

Breathing you so deeply I taste you and dance with your soul . . .
Dancing and singing and twirling like I have been spun with gold.

And when your spring drizzle becomes a torrential thunderstorm . . .
Ah . . . heavenly rain . . .
It's like I'm under a rainbow waterfall . . . being caressed
by a knowing, gentle breeze . . . flying with newborn butterflies
and singing with colorful birds in wind-stirred trees.

Your touch electrifies me though you have never touched me . . .
I smile with your smile without opening my eyes . . .
You are my destiny.

As I dream my beautiful dream of you . . . I smile!

~ FURMAN J. MEGGETT
www.cdbaby.com/fjm

Men! continued

WHAT BROUGHT US TOGETHER?

Julie and I originally got together as a result of a strong mutual attraction—physical, mental, and spiritual. This attraction turned into strong compatibility and has only deepened with time. Now, our successful marriage is just an extension of the way we've chosen to live our lives as a whole. That is—to live lives of love and service, to strive to do the best we can under whatever circumstances we find ourselves in and to encourage others to do the same, and to forgive ourselves (and others) when we fail in our tasks or objectives, and to make as the basis of our decisions whether our actions would result in a better world.

~ WILLIAM REMSEN

A POEM TO COVER HALF THE WORLD

She gently adjourns
        to her snug cocoon

And lingers an ocean
        away in sleep

Her faint undulations
        a vow to keep

Tugging and turning
        in tune with the moon.

> But here on my side
> Shrift half of the bed
> The blankets have fled
> So all night low tide.

~ KURT RIGHTMYER

Men!

My Rose, My Sharon

Dearest Sharon, I do love you,
For you are my wondrous wife.
Your soul is pure, your love is true,
You are the treasure of my life.

You've stood by me when times were hard,
You've cheered me on in good.
You've always won my soul's regard,
Your friendship is my food.

May God grant you protection,
May I live up to your dreams.
May life give deep satisfaction,
Our love be nourishing streams.

So keep in mind what I do send,
Especially when you feel laden.
You're my mate, my love, my best friend,
Brilliant flower of life's garden.

~ DILIP RANJITHA ABAYASEKARA

Mentoring

THE MAGIC OF MENTORS

*D*uring our lives, many people mentor us. They offer their guidance, wisdom and cheerleading. All are forms of support. Sometimes we do not even know when it happens. They suggest ideas, ask questions, and listen to our responses. For me, when people listen that closely, I am more careful of what I am saying. I notice that during later meetings they remember previous conversations, and ask me how my plans are coming along. This is typically followed by additional questions or simple suggestions.

Looking back, I was not aware that I was being mentored, I see that those people who have helped me most in my life truly had nothing to gain from it; no profit. They gave me things to think about and try. They were sincerely interested in my success. If I had planned for certain individuals to be my "mentors," they might not have been any of those people. However, their interest and influence in my life made it better. To value people and the wisdom they extend are the merits of mentoring.

Having, or being a mentor, requires your taking time to listen. It has been said that when the student is ready, the teacher appears. Whether you are the student—or the teacher—enjoy the magic of mentoring!

~ SUBMITTED BY JACK NICHOLS

Mid-Life for Women

Mid-life is when the growth of hair on our legs slows down.
This gives us plenty of time to care for
our newly acquired mustache.

Mid-life is when you go for a mammogram
and you realize that this is the only time someone
will ask you to appear topless.

In mid-life your memory starts to go.
In fact the only thing we can retain is water.

Mid-life means that you become more reflective . . .
You start pondering the "big" questions.

"What is life?"
"Why am I here?"

"How much Healthy Choice ice cream can I eat
before it's no longer a healthy choice?"

~ UNKNOWN

Military Relationships

TIPS AND IDEAS FOR KEEPING IT TOGETHER

- Make time every day for each other whether it's writing to or about your loved one, chatting online with them, or simply thinking about them. Keeping the lines of communication open in a long distance relationship is very important because that's all you have to interact with each other. Just letting your partner assume that you love and think of them often isn't enough.

- During your Internet rendezvous time, play a game online together. It can be very comforting to laugh and play together when you are apart.

- Send packages to each other. They may include something that reminded you of the other person, an article of clothing or a pillow with your cologne/perfume on it or handmade gifts.

- Call each other unexpectedly. Being surprised is something to look forward to in any relationship.

- Treat your partner with the respect you want for yourself. Just because you are physically apart doesn't mean that there are reasons not to trust each other.

- When your partner comes home, don't worry about the daily routine of doing the dishes, laundry or whatever else that could be set aside. Focus on doing something together. Intimacy is important, and many couples have found it productive to plan other fun activities together.

- Discuss expectations and concerns while you're together, but remember that it is called "leave" because it is a break from the harsh daily military life. Your partner doesn't need to come home and get patronized. If there are specific issues to talk about, write your thoughts down so that your point is clear before they get home, and then give it a while before approaching them. It is as equally important to discuss happy and exciting expectations with each other, as it is to deal with the non-positive ones.

~ BRETTANI WEBB
www.LovingYou.com

Mothers

Any mother could perform the jobs of several air traffic controllers with ease.

~ LISA ALTHER

She never quite leaves her children at home,
even when she doesn't take them along.

~ MARGARET CULKIN BANNING

I know how to do anything—I'm a mom.

~ ROSEANNE BARR

If evolution really works, how come mothers only have two hands?

~ MILTON BERLE

Some are kissing mothers and some are scolding mothers, but it is love just the same, and most mothers kiss and scold together.

~ PEARL S. BUCK
Author of Nobel Prize for Literature, 1938

You can fool all of the people some of the time,
and some of the people all of the time, but you Can't Fool Mom.

~ CAPTAIN PENNY'S LAW

A mother's love for her child is like nothing else in the world. It knows no law, no pity, it dares all things and crushes down remorselessly all that stands in its path.

~ AGATHA CHRISTIE

Mothers CONTINUED

There is a point where you aren't as much mom and daughter as you are adults and friends. It doesn't happen for everyone—but it did for Mom and me.

~ JAMIE LEE CURTIS

If you have never been hated by your child, you have never been a parent.

~ BETTE DAVIS

The heart of a mother is a deep abyss at the bottom of which you will always find forgiveness.

~ HONORÉ DE BALZAC

A suburban mother's role is to deliver children obstetrically once, and by car forever after.

~ PETER DE VRIES

My mother is a walking miracle . . .

~ LEONARDO DICAPRIO

My mother is a poem I'll never be able to write, though everything I write is a poem to my mother.

~ SHARON DOUBIAGO

Life began with waking up and loving my mother's face.

~ GEORGE ELIOT

Men are what their mothers made them.

~ RALPH WALDO EMERSON

Mothers <small>CONTINUED</small>

We are all connected to the one mother energy. From time to time we need to remind ourselves of that to feel our worth, how much we mean to those we know and to the universe.
~ LINDA FERBER

When I stopped seeing my mother with the eyes of a child, I saw the woman who helped me give birth to myself.
~ NANCY FRIDAY

Mother: the most beautiful word on the lips of mankind.
~ KAHLIL GIBRAN

The love of a parent for a child is the love that should grow towards separation.
~ KAHLIL GIBRAN

It's not easy being a mother. If it were easy, fathers would do it.
~ FROM THE TV SERIES *THE GOLDEN GIRLS*

God could not be everywhere, so he created mothers.
~ JEWISH PROVERB

The real religion of the world comes from women much more than from men—from mothers most of all, who carry the key of our souls in their bosoms.
~ OLIVER WENDELL HOLMES

Maternal love: a miraculous substance which God multiplies as He divides it.
~ VICTOR HUGO

Mothers

A mother is the truest friend we have, when trials heavy and sudden, fall upon us; when adversity takes the place of prosperity; when friends who rejoice with us in our sunshine desert us; when trouble thickens around us, still will she cling to us, and endeavor by her kind precepts and counsels to dissipate the clouds of darkness, and cause peace to return to our hearts.

~ WASHINGTON IRVING

Now, as always, the most automated appliance in a household is the mother.

~ BEVERLY JONES

A mother is a person who seeing there are only four pieces of pie for five people, promptly announces she never did care for pie.

~ TENNEVA JORDAN

When you are a mother, you are never really alone in your thoughts. A mother always has to think twice, once for herself and once for her child.

~ SOPHIA LOREN
Author of Women and Beauty

When momma's not happy—no one's happy!

~ DR. PHIL MCGRAW
Author of Life and Relationship Coach, www.DrPhil.com

Women's Liberation is just a lot of foolishness. It's the men who are discriminated against. They can't bear children. And no one's likely to do anything about that.

~ GOLDA MEIR

Mothers CONTINUED

Her children arise up, and call her blessed.
~ PROVERBS 31:28

The moment a child is born, the mother is also born. She never existed before. The woman existed, but the mother, never. A mother is something absolutely new.
~ RAJNEESH

An ounce of mother is worth a pound of priests.
~ SPANISH PROVERB

The phrase "working mother" is redundant.
~ JANE SELLMAN

Making the decision to have a child—it's momentous. It is to decide forever to have your heart go walking around outside your body.
~ ELIZABETH STONE

Motherhood has a very humanizing effect. Everything gets reduced to essentials.
~ MERYL STREEP, ACTRESS

Who is best taught? He who has first learned from his mother.
~ *THE TALMUD*

Mother is the name for God in the lips and hearts of little children.
~ WILLIAM MAKEPEACE THACKERAY
English novelist

Children are the sum of what mothers contribute to their lives.
~ UNKNOWN

A LOVE, MY LOVE

I laugh,
She smiles
A friend,
My playmate

I learn,
She teaches
A genius,
My almanac

I hurt,
She heals
A doctor,
My cure

I eat,
She's pleased
A chef,
My nutrition

I'm misunderstood
She understands
A psychologist,
My wisdom

I'm safe
She's strong
A hero,
My protection

I dream,
She encourages
A mentor,
My mom

~ALEKA MESAROS, AGE 15

Mothers

I REMEMBER MY MOTHER
She never sat straight upon a chair.
Three-quarters of her hung in the air,
Ready to jump up to do or to cook
Whatever I might overlook.

From New York to Detroit she drove alone.
No turnpikes then and no cell phone.
Just two little girls alone in the car,
Certain she could follow map or star.

And though we didn't always get along,
I remember how she could play any song,
And I expect to hear those tunes again,
When next we meet, just 'round the bend.

~ ROSALIE FERRER KRAMER
Speaker, poet, author of Dancing in the Dark: Things My Mother Never Told Me
www.authorsden.com/rosaliefkramer

MAMA MUSE
It's great to think back on how my mother and I have grown closer through the years. When I was little, I adored her. She was like God to me. I used to dream about the two of us being roommates when I went to college. Oh, how much fun we would have together! Then when I was in about fourth-fifth grade I went through the stage when I was "too cool" to be mommy's darling. If she ever tried to hug or kiss me I acted like, "Oh, yuck, get away!" Throughout my teenage years, she and I became close again. What a brat I had been for acting mean in my "tweens." No matter how naughty I was, Mom never stopped caring for me. She was unconditional in her love for me.

Mothers

We began our "mudder-dotter" adventures when I was three. I named it that when I was little because I couldn't pronounce "mother-daughter" and the name stuck as we made dates to do girlie girl things . . . manicures, facials, massages, tea parties. What we were really doing was bonding. My mother has one of the friendliest, most outgoing personalities there is. She treats others exactly how she wants them to treat her and she always sees the best in people. She believes in helping others live their dreams as she has helped me live mine. I can still hear her voice as she encourages me when I am frightened: "You can do it, you can do it, you're the greatest!"

What I've learned from my mother is to be real and authentic and to love grandly. Life is about communication and understanding. She is always telling me "you don't stop laughing because you grow old, you grow old because you stop laughing!" We laugh a lot.

My mom and I have a mother-daughter bond that will never be broken. She is my "Mama Muse," an inspiration and a motivation to me and others, although she'll tell you she is just "Mom Amuse." I want to follow in her footsteps by being the star she's taught me to be. Today we call ourselves the "Dynamic Duo." We are hosting TV and radio shows together, we write together, we speak together, and yes, we do have a house at college together. I can't imagine a greater love.

~ HEATHER BRITTANY
Actress on the TV series Veronica Mars

Editor's Note: Together, Heather and her mother, Cynthia Brian, write a column called Tea for Two—A Mother/Daughter Brew as well as host a popular radio program on World Talk Radio. www.star-style.com

Mothers <small>CONTINUED</small>

A Tribute to Mom

As I think back over the years when I was a kid,
It amazes me how Mom managed to do as much as she did.
Of course, she was the first one up and the last one to bed.
But even so, back in the 30s, life on the farm wasn't easy you know.
She sure had a lot of get up and go.
I remember that old washing machine,
with just a foot pedal and a push lever, she kept our clothes clean.
Not to mention the old wooden churn, with a crank and a creak
she made butter, about once a week.
With socks to darn and clothes to mend, work piled up, there was
    no end.
When spring came around there was a garden to plant and all
    summer to tend.
And when baby chicks arrived, the brooder house needed
    scrubbing
and the stove put back in. Canning time was really a chore.
Fruits and vegetables stacked high on the kitchen floor.
When Dad butchered, there was meat to cut and hams to cure,
Then lard to render, that was for sure.
Milking cows by hand was a daily routine,
like gathering eggs and separating milk from the cream.
The calves and pigs would get the skim,
with all these chores, she stayed pretty trim.
In summer time on many a hot day,
She pitched right in to help with the hay.
When shocking grain you could depend,
She'd keep up with the best of them.
In the fall of the year there was corn to pick,
T'would have made the average woman just sick.

Mothers

For 5 or 6 weeks from day till dark,
had to throw like the dickens before the snow starts.
In winter time when roads were blocked and schools were closed,
she knitted us warm mittens so we never froze.
With the snow to shovel and water to carry, she chopped wood too,
    when necessary.
On Saturday night we'd all get a bath,
we'd forget about school and all that math.
With hot water from the stove's reservoir
we could hardly wait to see a movie starring Dorothy Lamour.
But Mom had produce to sell and groceries to buy,
Lord knows she had little time to sit down and cry.
She just took things in stride, one day at a time.
And never seemed to tire when in her prime.
Yes, these are just a few of the thing my momma did,
and still found time to love all seven kids.

~ YOUR SON, VERNON

Editor's Note: Vernon Lundquist, country singer and the eldest of the seven Iowa farm kids. Written about and for his mother Nellie Reimers Lundquist, beloved grandmother of Sheryl Roush, editor of this publication.

Music

Poetry is music written for the human voice.

~ MAYA ANGELOU
American poet, writer, and actress

Music was my refuge. I could crawl into the space between the notes and curl my back to loneliness.

~ MAYA ANGELOU
Author of Gather Together in My Name

Music washes away from the soul the dust of everyday life.

~ BERTHOLD AUERBACH

Its language is a language which the soul alone understands, but which the soul can never translate.

~ ARNOLD BENNETT

Love is a friendship set to music.

~ JOSEPH CAMPBELL
Author, philosopher

There is in soul's a sympathy with sounds:
And as the mind is pitch'd the ear is pleased
With melting airs, or martial, brisk or grave;
Some chord in unison with what we hear
Is touch'd within us, and the heart replies.

~ WILLIAM COWPER

Music is the literature of the heart; it commences where speech ends.

~ ALPHONSE DE LAMARTINE

Music CONTINUED

Love is the harmony of two souls singing together.
~ GREGORY J. P. GODEK
Romance author

Take a music bath once or twice a week for a few seasons. You will find it is to the soul what a water bath is to the body.
~ OLIVER WENDELL HOLMES

Music is love in search of a word.
~ SIDNEY LANIER

Every single one of us can do things that no one else can do—can love things that no one else can love. We are like violins. We can be used for doorstops, or we can make music. You know what to do.
~ BARBARA SHER

Music fills the infinite between two souls. This has been muffled by the mist of our daily habits.
~ RABINDRANATH TAGORE

Music is the shorthand of emotion.
~ LEO TOLSTOY

Music is a higher revelation than philosophy.
~ LUDWIG VON BEETHOVEN

Music is the mediator between the spiritual and the sensual life.
~ LUDWIG VAN BEETHOVEN

Music is what feelings sound like.
~ UNKNOWN

Nature

The power of nature to calm, heal and inspire is enormous for those that take the time to look. The flaming clouds of a summer sunset; the buttercup yellow of a full moon rising on a cloudless night; mist sweeping up a valley; bird calls at dawn, all lift me beyond the present, even if sometimes only for a moment.

~ ANNE FRODSHAM
Horticulturist and nature lover

Go outside. Leave the sidewalks behind.

~ CATH KACHUR
Speaker, artist, www.HumanTuneUp.com

Snowflakes are one of Nature's most fragile things, but just look what they can do when they stick together.

~ VERNA KELLEY

Like water, be gentle and strong. Be gentle enough to follow the natural paths of the earth, and strong enough to rise up and reshape the world.

~ BRENDA PETERSON

Nature is beautiful. It is the basis of our survival. No nature, no us.

~ ALISON J. ROUSH
8 years old and the saviour of all things living.

There is a wonderful law of nature that the three things we crave most—happiness, freedom, and peace of mind—are always attained by giving them to someone else.

~ UNKNOWN

You can't get much closer to God than this!

~ WARDENE WEISSER
Nature photographer

Old Maid Next Door

I found my true love right next door . . . literally! I live in the country and was out "mowing" the pastures. The house next door was up for sale and no one was maintaining the property–so I was mowing the two foot tall field next to my property. Mowing this type of grass is not fun or easy and so I was "dressed" for the occasion.

Being a red head with sun sensitive skin . . . I was all covered up on a hot day in June. My totally appropriate outfit was a wide brim sun hat, wrap around sun glasses, a turtle neck, stretch pants, an old pair of after ski boots and of course work gloves and oh by the way . . . no makeup!

As I was mowing, a car pulled into my neighbor's driveway and out hopped two men. They were "surveying" the property and checking out the barn. One gentleman, waved me down. He introduced himself as Steve Sparks and introduced his friend Wes to me. He asked why I was mowing "his property"? I said the field was too high and I was concerned about bugs and critters!

We chatted and had a fun conversation and off I went, back to mowing and Steve and his friend went about their way. Later I found out, Wes said to Steve . . . "good luck with the old maid next door!"

Well, almost two years have gone by since that day and Steve and I have been dating for over a year, are incredibly in love and both feel as though we have found our true soulmate and are talking about joining our lives together this year. (I am planning on surprising him with the original outfit he met me in on our wedding day!) He still kids me about "cleaning up pretty well"! We have an underground tunnel from my home to his . . . only kidding . . . just a well-worn walking path. So much for the old maid next door!

~ MARGUERITE HAM
The Old Maid, Speaker, author, coach, www.memorease.com

Parenting

You see much more of your children once they leave home.
~ LUCILLE BALL

To bring up a child in the way he should go, travel that way yourself once in a while.
~ JOSH BILLINGS

Don't expect your children to do anything you won't do for yourself.
~ COLETTE CARLSON
Speaker, contributing author of Conversations on Success

There are two lasting bequests we can give our children. One is roots. The other is wings.
~ HODDING CARTER, JR.

In spite of the six thousand manuals on child raising in the bookstores, child raising is still a dark continent and no one really knows anything. You just need a lot of love and luck—and, of course, courage.
~ BILL COSBY
Author of Fatherhood

No matter how calmly you try to referee, parenting will eventually produce bizarre behavior, and I'm not talking about the kids.
~ BILL COSBY
Author of Fatherhood

It would seem that something which means poverty, disorder and violence every single day should be avoided entirely, but the desire to beget children is a natural urge.
~ PHYLLIS DILLER

Parenting CONTINUED

There actually was a time I was a perfect parent and I knew all the answers—then, the first baby came along and suddenly I realized I didn't even know what the questions were.

~ RITA EMMETT, RECOVERING PROCRASTINATOR
Author of The Procrastinating Child: A Handbook for Adults to Help Children Stop Putting Things Off, *www.RitaEmmett.com*

Don't worry that children never listen to you; worry that they are always watching you.

~ ROBERT FULGHUM

Parents often talk about the younger generation as if they didn't have anything to do with it.

~ HAIM GINOTT

The beauty of "spacing" children many years apart lies in the fact that parents have time to learn the mistakes that were made with the older ones—which permits them to make exactly the opposite mistakes with the younger ones.

~ SYDNEY J. HARRIS

Your children need your presence more than your presents.

~ REVEREND JESSE JACKSON

If there is anything that we wish to change in the child, we should first examine it and see whether it is not something that could better be changed in ourselves.

~ CARL JUNG
Integration of the Personality, *1939*

Parenting CONTINUED

People either imitate or make vows not to be like their parents.

~ CATH KACHUR
Speaker, artist, www.HumanTuneUp.com

Whenever I held my newborn baby in my arms, I used to think that what I said and did to him could have an influence not only on him but on all whom he met, not only for a day or a month or a year, but for all eternity—a very challenging and exciting thought for a mother.

~ ROSE KENNEDY

You will always be your child's favorite toy.

~ VICKI LANSKY
Trouble-Free Travel with Children, *1991*

Insanity is hereditary—you get it from your kids.

~ SAM LEVENSON

If I had my child to raise all over again,
I'd build self-esteem first, and the house later.
I'd finger-paint more, and point the finger less.
I would do less correcting and more connecting.
I'd take my eyes off my watch, and watch with my eyes.
I'd take more hikes and fly more kites.
I'd stop playing serious, and seriously play.
I would run through more fields and gaze at more stars.
I'd do more hugging and less tugging.

~ DIANE LOOMANS
Speaker, author of If I Had My Child To Raise Over Again

Parenting CONTINUED

It's not only children who grow. Parents do too. As much as we watch to see what our children do with their lives, they are watching us to see what we do with ours. I can't tell my children to reach for the sun. All I can do is reach for it, myself.

~ JOYCE MAYNARD

Mama does everything for the baby, who responds by saying Dada first.

~ MIGNON MCLAUGHLIN
Author of The Second Neurotic's Notebook

It's never too late to be a better parent. Start today. Model the behavior you wish to see in your children. Discipline with wisdom and gentleness. Love freely and openly, expressing often and in many ways how you cherish and value each of your children, just as God treasures each of us.

~ MARY MANIN MORRISSEY
Author of Life Keys

Sing out loud in the car even, or especially, if it embarrasses your children.

~ MARILYN PENLAND

Like all parents, my husband and I just do the best we can, hold our breath and hope we've set aside enough money for our kid's therapy.

~ MICHELLE PFEIFFER

You have a lifetime to work, but children are only young once.

~ POLISH PROVERB

Teach your children to choose the right path, and when they are older, they will remain upon it.

~ PROVERBS 22:6

Parenting CONTINUED

It's sad that children cannot know their parents when they were younger; when they were loving, courting, and being nice to one another. By the time children are old enough to observe, the romance has all too often faded or gone underground.

~ VIRGINIA SATIR

If there is love, there is no such thing as being too tough with a child.

~ SANDRA SCHRIFT
Grandmother, career coach, www.schrift.com

Having kids—the responsibility of rearing good, kind, ethical, responsible human beings—the biggest job anyone can embark on. Like any risk, you have to take a leap of faith and ask lots of wonderful people for their help and guidance. I thank God every day for giving me the opportunity to parent.

~ MARIA KENNEDY SHRIVER SCHWARTZENEGGER
O Magazine *by Oprah*

Parents must get across the idea that "I love you always, but sometimes I do not love your behavior."

~ AMY VANDERBILT
Author, authority on manners and etiquette

Before I got married I had six theories about bringing up children; now I have six children, and no theories.

~ JOHN WILMOT

When you put faith, hope and love together, you can raise positive kids in a negative world.

~ ZIG ZIGLAR
Motivational speaker, author

Passion

Passion is a first kiss and a last.
Passion is a steaming "Cup of Joe."
Passion is entering the 10K—just because.
Passion is creating life in your likeness.
Passion is volunteering at the shelter.
Passion is loving the beach on an overcast day.
Passion is cradling a newborn kitten.
Passion is teaching a child to read the printed word.
Passion is placing a stroke of magenta on a white canvas.
Passion is not letting the cancer win.
Passion is listening to the same CD thirty times in a row.
Passion is noticing the smile on a stranger's face.
Passion is the next keystroke of an overdue letter.
Passion is discovering love after the infatuation.
Passion is fitting together the jigsaw of life.

~ LEE A. BARRON
Publisher, author

Today a new sun rises for me;
everything lives,
everything is animated,
everything seems to speak to me of my passion,
everything invites me to cherish it.

~ ANNE DE LENCLOS

Finding your passion is connecting the dots between your head
and your heart.

~ MARIA MARSALA
www.ElevatingYou.com

Passion CONTINUED

Be a person of passion. Feel passion for something, someone.
To go through life without a passion is like not experiencing the fullest in you.

~ SANDRA SCHRIFT
Career coach, www.schrift.com

Passion is energy. Feel the power that comes from focusing on what excites you. Your true passion should feel like breathing; it's that natural.

~ OPRAH WINFREY

5 STEPS TO FINDING YOUR PASSION

True happiness comes when you do what you are most passionate about. Uncover your true passion—and start living it!

1. Get Quiet
2. Become Sensitive to Your Environment
3. Answer a Series of Questions: *What interest, passion or desire are you most afraid of admitting to yourself and others? What do you love about yourself? Who do you know that's doing something you'd like to do? Describe yourself doing it. How could you make the world a better place for yourself and others? What's stopping you from moving forward with exploring your passion?*
4. Go on a Treasure Hunt
5. Take a Risk

~ CHERYL RICHARDSON
Author, speaker, guest on Oprah Winfrey's Lifestyle Makeovers: How to Find Your Passion

Now Begin

Beneath the degrees, titles, accomplishments,
What is inside, to be discovered at your core?
What is your unique and special spark?
Buried deep, neglected, chosen to ignore

Seeking to please whomever
Drowning out pure longings of your heart
Struggling, freezing, suffocating
Until finally, you choose to start

Whispers from the spirit
Souls songs from deep within
After dancing, stranger among strangers,
Claim it! Your life! Now begin!

~ JULIE JORDAN SCOTT
www.5passions.com

Patriotism

*S*ome people are afraid of flying. Most of us have had a flight that we wish we had never taken. As a flight attendant, there were hundreds of flights and the worst fears were mechanical problems or bad weather. She had trust in the airplanes, the pilots, and the air-traffic controllers to get her and her passengers safely to their destinations. She knew flying was safer than driving her car on the California freeways to work. Then September 11, 2001 happened and everything changed.

Leann had worked a United Airlines flight from Boston to San Francisco on September 9th. Afterward she had some days off, and flew home to Orlando on September 10th. Then came the devastating morning of 9-11 and everyone was grounded. She listened to the news reports and saw the pictures of the airplanes over and over again; United Flight 175, which originated in Boston, crashed into the south tower of the World Trade Center. There was the explosion and a ball of fire and so many lives were gone. Twelve of those who perished that day were her flying partners. By one account, the hijackers who boarded the airplane in Boston started killing flight attendants in order to get the pilots out of the cockpit. It could have been her. She sat at home for several days thinking about her career choice. She did not sign up for this! She was willing to take her chances; however, terrorism was not a part of the plan.

A few days later she was told to report to work and did not know if she could do it. Would she be able to even walk onto that airplane? Would she be able to stand in front of the passengers and show them the safety information? A flight attendant never shows fear and is responsible for keeping the passengers calm. Would she be able to act when action was needed?

Patriotism CONTINUED

Flying to her home base in San Francisco was the first step. On this flight she would be a passenger, but she needed to wear her uniform in order to go to work when she arrived in San Francisco. When Leann walked with the flight crew down the United concourse at the Orlando airport, passengers at each gate stood up and applauded as they passed by. This outpouring of appreciation and respect was a turning point for her. These people, as well as hundreds of thousands of people all over the country, were stranded. Although airplanes had been turned into weapons of mass destruction, America needed to keep flying, and flight attendants had to return to work. She boarded the airplane and made that first flight—and on to the next flight—and the next. Leann faced her fear determined to do her job in a profession that had changed forever.

~ JACK NICHOLS

Patriotism CONTINUED

UNITED WE STAND
IF
(In memory of September 11th, 2001)

If everyone is glued to the news
Worried about what is happening far over seas,
If everyone is trying to find a few clues
As to find why someone far away would now be pleased,
If the people around you are angry or upset
At the events that have taken place,
And wanting to help others that they have never met
Which prior in our country was an unusual case.
If our elected leader vows retribution
For the awful deeds that were done,
If he is determined to find the means in our constitution
Promising that those responsible will never again have fun,
If the rest of the world shows us compassion
Backing our nation all the way,
Each lending help in their own fashion
Uniting the world with the event of one awful day.
If those found guilty are hunted down
And prosecuted for their crimes,
Will there still be on everyone's face a frown
A lingering reminder of these horrid times?
If it takes a tragedy so great
To unite people everywhere,
Then let us all stand together before it's too late
And show the world that Americans do care!

~ SERINA ROUSH, AGE 17

Pets

FURRY WISDOM

*O*ur animals love us in many ways. Some ways are the obvious running around in circles, woofing madly or the bird's welcome whistle when we come home. Sometimes they love us with a precious intricate wisdom that can be easy to miss if we don't attribute to them the depth of awareness and intentionality they truly possess.

A few years ago, recently divorced I was stoically keeping it all together, just barely. I was making it, I really was and that in itself was a miracle. One day I was exhausted and sat down, just for a second. In that second and in one fluid movement my big tabby cat hopped into my lap, started his deep rumbling purr and somehow managed to maneuver his long, fifteen pound body into a position with his back firmly pressed against my front and the top of his head snug under my chin. We sat like that for a few minutes his love pouring into me.

My tears started slowly, at first in deep gratitude for his presence and being so loved and later in great sobs in huge relief from the stress and realization that we were going to be okay. As soon as I was done crying and he was good and wet he jumped down. His job was all done. He was completely aware that I needed to let go and the fastest way was to line up his spine with mine and pour the love in. Clear, compassionate furry wisdom!

~ANUPO JOY
Animal intuitive, author of Mystical Awakenings, *www.AnupoJoy.com*

LESSONS FROM THE BARNYARD

*O*ver the years, people have laughed at me because of my great fondness for animals. I have been called "the Chicken Lady" (because I raised chickens to earn money for college), "a female Dr. Doolittle" (for my menagerie), and other names, some not so kind.

Pets <small>CONTINUED</small>

I'm undeterred.

Affection is kinship with another, an emotional bond, a true fondness from the heart. I believe that many humans are programmed to give tenderness, but don't know how to receive it. They are afraid to open themselves, or they cynically view expressions of endearment with suspicion, suspecting ulterior motives. For some, an undemanding animal gives us permission to both give and receive unconditional love. My animals have taught me some of my most important lessons in human relationships—compassion, love, empathy, and perseverance. Animals feel emotional bonds just as we humans do, and they are not afraid to exhibit their affections for one another and their human friends.

I have always marveled that I can come home from a completely terrible day, looking like I've been in a thunderstorm, smelling like I've been on a garbage truck, and be greeted by my dogs, horses, and goats as if I were a queen arriving for a great occasion.

Can you imagine how wonderful our relationships would be if we allowed ourselves to do this with people? To experience the simple pleasure of demonstrating our affection when loved ones arrive home by jumping up and down, barking, and dancing in circles? Celebrating their joys or participating in a good cry instead offering "solutions" to their problems? As George Eliot said, "Animals are such agreeable friends; they ask no questions, and they pass no criticisms."

Take a lesson from all God's creatures. Show your fondness for this world we live in. The more you care, the more love you will encounter. Pass it on.

~ CYNTHIA BRIAN
Speaker, author of the New York Times *best-selling* Chicken Soup for the Gardener's Soul, Be the Star You Are!, The Business of Show Business *and others. www.star-style.com*

Prayer

For the eyes of the Lord are on the righteous and his ears are attentive to their prayer.
~ I PETER 3:12, WOMEN'S DEVOTIONAL BIBLE 2, NEW INT'L VERSION

There are three answers to prayers: Yes, no, and wait
~ EMILY B. DESHAZO

Do not be anxious about anything, but in everything, by prayer and petition, with thanksgiving, present your requests to God. And the peace of God, which transcends all understanding, will guard your hearts and your minds in Jesus Christ.
~ PHILIPPIANS 4:6–7, WOMEN'S DEVOTIONAL BIBLE 2, NEW INT'L VERSION

Thank God for this glorious day. I shall rise, rejoice and be glad in it. Thank you for every way in which I experience your Love—through giving, sharing and receiving. Use my life. I am your messenger.
~ SHERYL ROUSH
Speaker, author of Sparkle-Tudes! *and* Heart of A Mother, *www.SparklePresentations.com*

"Modeh Ani"
"I am grateful before you."
These are the first words you are to say in the morning in traditional Jewish life. When you start the day being grateful, the hectic morning rush (kids, dog, sandwiches, backpacks) falls into perspective . . . (if you have a moment to think about it).
~ LINDA KAPLAN SPITZ, MD

Do not make prayer a monologue—make it a conversation.
~ UNKNOWN

Prayer continued

God's answers are wiser than our prayers.

~ UNKNOWN

MY DAILY PRAYER

If I can do some good today,
If I can serve along life's way,
If I have something helpful say,
Lord, show me how.
If I can right a human wrong,
If I can help to make one strong,
If I can cheer with smile or song,
Lord, show me how.
If I can aid one in distress,
If I can make a burden less,
If I can spread more happiness,
Lord, show me how.

~ UNKNOWN

FIVE FINGERS OF PRAYER

1. Your thumb is nearest to you. Begin your prayers by praying for those closest to you. They are the easiest to remember.
2. The next finger is the pointing finger. Pray for those who teach, instruct and heal. This includes teachers, doctors, and ministers. They need support and wisdom in pointing others in the right direction. Keep them in your prayers.
3. The next finger is the tallest finger. It reminds us of our leaders. Pray for the president, leaders in business and industry and administrators. These people shape our nation and guide public opinion. They need God's guidance.

4. The fourth finger is our ring finger. Surprising to many is the fact that this is our weakest finger, as any piano teacher will testify. It should remind us to pray for those who are weak, in trouble or in pain. They need your prayers day and night. You cannot pray too much for them.

5. And lastly comes our little finger; the smallest finger of all, which is where we should place ourselves in relation to God and others. As the Bible says, "The least shall be the greatest among you. The last shall be first." Your pinkie should remind you to pray for yourself. By the time you have prayed for the other four groups, your own needs will be put into proper perspective and you will be able to pray for yourself more effectively.

~ ANONYMOUS

OUR PRAYER FOR OUR CHILDREN

Children of the Light—as you walk into your school, down the hall, into your classroom, to the playground, into your library, and lunch places—we promise to hold you in Love's embrace and massively comfort you with our watchful thoughts and prayers. We promise to remember that you come from Love. You go in Love, speak in Love, and move in Love. You ARE Love. Thank you for who you are.

The appearance of your smallness does not fool us into thinking that you are vulnerable. We see your spiritual strength and power as your divine inheritance. We see you in Love's embrace, forever safe. We know that the angels of care are causing you to think according to your true identity, to be in your appointed place of dignity, worth, preciousness, and power—protected while you go about your business of good. We are with you.

Prayer CONTINUED

You, our cherished children, are in the healing light of Love. We want you to know that we are assuring you by our continual watchful and loving thoughts for you. Our prayers will be the footprints of Love all around you, throughout the day. You will feel them. You will know them. They will be present with you, keeping you safe and secure. We will keep our sacred watch for you. You—all of you—are our children. Not one of you is outside our love.

Please know how much we care. We promise to pause for moments throughout our day to remember who you are—to honor your divinity. Please feel our hugs surrounding you, our kisses celebrating you. Please hear our messages of love for you.

Let us whisper to you this prayer of Love. Feel it to your toes. Let your heart sing with happiness, play, and safety. Hear our prayer. You are irreplaceable. You are magnificent. You are our wonders. Go in Love's way. Love is holding you in Her care, every waking moment, even as you rest your sweet head, on Love's pillow of peace. We love you and always will.

~ SHANNON PECK

Co-founder of TheLoveCenter, a non-profit educational organization dedicated to bringing all humanity into the heart of Love. She is a co-author of The Love You Deserve, Liberating Your Magnificence *with husband Dr. Scott Peck.*
© Copyright 1999 by Shannon Peck

Pregnancy

Q: I'm two months pregnant now. When will my baby move?
A: With any luck, right after he finishes college.

Q: My wife is five months pregnant and so moody that sometimes she's borderline irrational.
A: So, what's your question?

Q: My childbirth instructor says it's not pain I'll feel during labor, but pressure. Is she right?
A: Yes, in the same way that a tornado might be called an air current.

Q: When is the best time to get an epidural?
A: Right after you find out you're pregnant.

Q: Our baby was born last week. When will my wife begin to feel and act normal again?
A: When the kids are in college.

Think of stretch marks as pregnancy service stripes.
~ JOYCE ARMOR

You should never say anything to a woman that even remotely suggests that you think she's pregnant unless you can see an actual baby emerging from her at that moment.
~ DAVE BARRY
Author of Things That It Took Me 50 Years to Learn

Pregnancy

Don't wreck a sublime chocolate experience by feeling guilty. Chocolate isn't like premarital sex. It will not make you pregnant. And it always feels good.

~ LORA BRODY
Author of Growing Up on the Chocolate Diet

There are three reasons for breast-feeding: the milk is always at the right temperature; it comes in attractive containers; and the cat can't get it.

~ IRENA CHALMERS

By far the most common craving of pregnant women is not to be pregnant.

~ PHYLLIS DILLER

If pregnancy were a book they would cut the last two chapters.

~ NORA EPHRON
Author of Heartburn, *1983*

It is now possible for a flight attendant to get a pilot pregnant.

~ RICHARD J. FERRIS
President of United Airlines

The spiritual quality of earth: eternally pregnant and containing in its fertility the unwritten cipher of cosmic lore.

~ LADY FRIEDA HARRIS
English artist

If nature had arranged that husbands and wives should have children alternatively, there would never be more than three in a family.

~ LAWRENCE HOUSMAN

Prosperity

1. *Cleansing and Elimination*—The first stage of creating prosperity is releasing. This may mean old patterns, thoughts, beliefs, losing weight, clothes, dust-collectors around the house, books, clutter, even relationships that no longer serve us.

2. *Vacuum and Circulation*—By releasing the old, we make space for the new, and better. A vacuum is then created to be filled back up again. Circulation begins again.

3. *Order and Expansion*—Only by having a sense of order and organization can there be an expansion. Clean up the clutter, get organized and be ready to receive more.

4. *Forgiveness and Release*—By forgiving those who we believe have done us wrong somehow, we release the negative energy from that experience or those people. Often the ones we truly need to forgive is ourselves. Through this forgiveness, we have a greater purity in our hearts, and less stress.

5. *"Give-ability" and Tithing*—Our ability to receive more is directly linked to our ability to give. We can offer our time, energy, talents, earnings, compassion . . . True giving is without any expectation of receiving.

6. *Receptivity*—With all this releasing, and giving, our hearts and lives are now ready to receive. The space is made available in our homes, work environments and hearts. By releasing old love relationships, we're ready to find new ones, fresh starts. By giving clothes away, our closets can hold more, newer styles and colors that make us feel better about ourselves.

Prosperity continued

7. Creativity—With fresh minds and environments, new ideas are inspired to grace us. Perhaps pursue a newfound inspiration for reading or writing new books, poetry, recipes, sports, gardening, crafts or hobbies.

8. Love—The law supports loving others, as best and as unconditionally as we are able. It may be through prayer for those we know need support, peace, condolences, or healing. By giving love first we receive it. It comes back to us from other sources, too.

These eight steps, or laws, enable us to receive, give and share more of the Universal love and Divine guidance in our lives, which attracts more prosperity.

~ SHERYL ROUSH
Speaker, author of Sparkle-Tudes! *and* Heart of A Mother, *www.SparklePresentations.com*

Raising Fearless Women

A Guide for Parents and Influencers of Young Women Everywhere

*F*ear. What is it and why does it stop us?

In my 20s, I read Frank Herbert's *Dune* trilogy and remember its hero Paul Atreides saying, "Fear is the mind killer." I agree. I've seen how fear stops us by killing our wills and our minds. When stuck in fear, we can no longer think; we simply respond.

On the other hand, fear can make us strong and even courageous. Because of this, I don't advocate making sure that young girls around us never have to deal with fear. Instead, let's teach them to not allow fear to stifle them or kill their minds. For fear breeds courage and courage can propel them to excellence, to move fearlessly through their lives.

Yet how does a young girl learn to move through the fear and not get stuck in it? I believe it depends on the significant adults in her life. What these adults say and do in the earliest years affect her forever.

OUR FIRST BORN ERIN

I waited until I was in my 30s to have children. From the moment of conception, I knew I was pregnant. I felt my body creating, molding, and changing. As my eagerly anticipated daughters took on personalities both before their births and after, their inner force was unmistakable. I knew I would devote my energy to them exclusively for many years.

When my firstborn Erin arrived in 1980, my life as a career college teacher changed dramatically. Our family moved from the city to a small town several states away. I suddenly found myself in a rural setting with a newborn and no family and close friends nearby. This led to lots of time and a strong desire to raise this baby to become a woman of significance. I asked, "How can I ensure she will learn to

Raising Fearless Women <small>CONTINUED</small>

fearlessly control her own destiny?" My answer was to talk to Erin as if she already *was* that fearless woman.

Starting in her first hours outside the womb, my husband and I looked straight into her eyes and told her what a wonder she was, how she could be whatever she wanted. We pledged our support and love, but not our rule. She would be allowed to decide for herself how to live her life. (Saying this to a newborn reflects my belief that infants can understand intentions and messages at a deep, innate level.)

As Erin grew up, we realized she had a strong sense of self and we honored it—not breaking her spirit but nurturing and respecting it. *Who she was* mattered immensely to us. We constantly told her so with our actions and our words.

When she talked, we'd make eye contact, let her express herself openly, listen fully, and respond with respect. By doing that, she *did* have important things to say and she *did* say them with confidence—a self-fulfilling prophecy. Many people assume that kind of confidence is stubbornness. We did not. As a result, Erin never felt inadequate or incapable. She felt safe to be herself. Even today, Erin remembers feeling that way as a child. And in her darkest hours, she knew she was loved and cherished and respected. She never questioned her worth.

OUR SECOND BORN HEATHER

Heather arrived when Erin was two and a half. Her big sister was thrilled with this new baby who looked at her with awe and joy from the start. During their preschool years, they played together and slept in the same bed. For a time, we even had a "family" bed until the girls decided they wanted their own room—an issue we never forced because we trusted it would show up in its own time.

Of course, the ramblings of a toddler can be perceived as just ramblings. But we learned that listening leads to connections and conceptual thinking—traits we always reinforced. For example, while driving with her dad in his truck, Heather saw a car that was the same make and model of one I'd driven, but with slight differences in color. When this toddler commented about the car, her dad replied, "That's a good observation, Heather." Even at age three, she still remembers how good it felt to have her dad believe in her abilities and *tell her so*. That turned into *a belief in herself* that would be put to a terrible test a few years loater. She calls it her foundation, a belief that saved her life.

Growing up, these two young girls never felt afraid of the dark or cried themselves to sleep. At the end of each day, they enjoyed feelings of peace, companionship, security. I can't tell you that fights between them never happened, but no matter what, they always *knew* they couldn't lose the love of their parents because of something they did. Validated and affirmed, they felt unconditionally "okay"—no strings attached, no exceptions.

DIVORCE AND REMARRIAGE

In 1989, when Erin was eight and Heather six, our family moved back to the city. That's also when my unhappy husband filed for divorce. We conversed with the girls to reassure them that this adult issue was not a result of anything they had or hadn't done. Although Erin was furious and outwardly expressive, she was secure enough in herself to be openly angry and not fearful of our wrath. Heather was more reflective and processed her feelings internally. She never believed the divorce it was her fault, but she felt truly sad about the loss. The three of us moved to a new neighborhood, and the girls were able to make new friends and succeed in school right away— a testament to their resilient spirit in spite of their broken hearts.

Thankfully, the girls and I lived close to their dad and saw him often, living out my belief that maintaining our friendship was the only way to act. He continued to support his daughters and be part of their lives, as he does to this day. Our divorce helped our daughters understand that life can change around them, but *who a person is* remains constant. So does deserving love and respect.

That same year, a new man named Rodger surprisingly came into my life. He had two children he had raised—16-year-old Blake and 14-year-old Amber. On our first date, we took all the kids roller skating. They liked each other immediately and before long it became apparent the chemistry was right to create a new, blended family. That December, Rodger and I married, even though people around us said it was "too soon." Did I know what the heck I was doing? I thought so, because I knew this marriage came with a strong foundation. That belief was confirmed just a few short weeks after our wedding.

A BUMP ON THE HEAD

In mid-January, 1990, we noticed a troubling bump on Heather's forehead that kept growing. She stayed home from school and felt tremendously tired. For such an active, athletic child, this behavior was highly unusual. The doctor said she'd just bumped her head, but I knew there was more. Shortly after, our chiropractor did a blood test and, knowing I was alarmed, expedited getting the results. He stood at our door the same evening, lab results in hand, and said, "This is way out of my hands. I've already called Children's Hospital. God bless you."

The doctors at Children's Hospital confirmed a diagnosis of acute lymphoblastic leukemia. We listened to rounds of specialists talk about treatment plans and protocols. In the process, we witnessed the courage of those in our new family as everyonefaced the reality of Heather's illness. Blake even slept on the floor of her hospital room to take care of his new little sister. Overnight, these four kids became a family; any difficulties in "blending" disappeared. Heather needed us all.

Fortunately, Heather beat the cancer that first go-around and it went into remission. She went back to school, and except for her treatment and her bald head, she was like all the other kids and could do all the activities they did. For the next four and a half years, we lived our lives quite normally.

Then a few days before Heather's twelfth birthday, I noticed bruises on her body. Knowing that deep, yellow bruises can be a sign of leukemia, I put my intuition on high alert. When we went to a studio for a family photograph, the photographer kept adjusting the lights and saying. "I just can't get the light right on Heather's face. She's a little yellow." I didn't sleep at all that night. At the doctor's office the next day, we learned that the cancer had returned.

FAMILY VIGILANCE

Our family focused on Heather's illness almost exclusively. I even took a leave from work to sleep in the window "bed" in her room at Children's Hospital. After about a week of 24/7 vigilance, Heather turned to me and said, "Mommy, I need you to go back to work."

"But Mommy wants to stay with you, sweetie. I'm fine. Work can wait. You're more important."

"No, Mommy. I need your energy and you don't have any. You get energy from doing your work. Go back to your job and then you'll have energy to see me."

So, I went back to work and visited Heather every evening. We laughed and talked and I brought her my energy. That's when I learned one of the biggest lessons of my life—I could be a better mom when I had a job I loved and a life outside of the home. And to get through this crisis, I needed to be the *best* mother I could be.

Heather had always been able to tell me what she needed. It was no different during her hospitalizations. Even at such a young age, she knew exactly who she was and what was happening to her. She asked questions and took control over her care. When the doctors would ask me, "What do you want to do?" I'd look at Heather and let them know they needed to ask *her* those questions. Of course, as parents we played a critical advisory role, but her input was not optional. It was her body; she would have a say in every decision.

As a new year dawned, it became apparent we needed a more drastic treatment or we'd lose Heather. So we prepared for a bone marrow transplant and Erin's marrow proved to be a match. She offered her kidneys and liver, too, if Heather needed them. Our 14-year-old daughter felt confident about the sacrifice she would have to make—and made it gladly to save her sister's life. The transplant—what we have come to call Heather's second birthday—took place on February 8, 1995.

The year that followed was full of unknowns. Unknown viruses, graft versus host disease, and strange reactions in a body with a weakened immune system. While her family watched like spectators, Heather was the only one who knew she would survive the full blur of treatments and home health care and re-hospitalizations.

The next year Heather returned to school, a small, frail teen who was also bald. Kids taunted her and asked, "Are you a boy or a girl?" In class, when the other kids would act out, she could quiet them all with a look. She desperately wanted to be normal and wouldn't allow anyone or anything to take that away from her again. Her teachers called her a powerhouse, not in stature but in will. She firmly knew who she was and so did everyone else.

APPRECIATING THE GIFT OF LIFE

Naturally, Heather's illness has given us a deeper appreciation for the gift of life *with no guarantees attached*. I wanted to reinforce that appreciation and set an example for learning two enduring principles:

it's the obligation of those who have to give to those who don't have, and, nothing creates gratefulness more than helping someone less fortunate than ourselves.

That thinking led us to a group called "Mexican Medical," which has built medical clinics and churches all over Baja California. Our church in Colorado made annual treks to work in one of these clinics, so in 1998, Erin and Heather and I excitedly headed to San Quintin, Mexico, to help out. We spent several afternoons in migrant camps playing with the children, sometimes taking them out of the camp to get the medical attention they needed. Erin was studying Spanish, which came in handy.

There, something courageous happened.

When we first entered the camp, several Mexican children surrounded Heather who still had to wear leg braces and walked with a limp. They quickly found a place for her to sit. No strangers to pain and suffering, they didn't shy away from her disability, nor did they ignore it. *They simply wanted to take care of her.* Heather's presence gave these fearless migrant children a gift—a chance to be kind and to serve another human being. And they rose to the task with dignity and respect.

The second year, Amber joined the three of us in Mexico. Our giving two weeks for three years to the grateful people there molded and changed our lives forever. Today, Erin works in Watts, a poor suburb of Los Angeles, California, following four years in South Central L.A. She teaches inner city kids that they have choices. Always, she treats them with dignity and respect. In some cases, she's the first person in their lives to ever do that.

Erin and her fellow teachers even took a class of fourth and fifth graders from her school in Watts to Ghana, Africa, to help them discover where they came from and expand their world view. When I told her how proud I was that she would help these kids "get out of the ghetto," she calmly (but with authority) told me I was wrong. "I don't want them to leave the community," she said. "I want them to stay there and change it."

Heather has grown into a strong woman. In May, 2006, she graduated with a bachelor's degree in History and Italian from the University of Colorado. Heather spent her junior year in Italy, living with families in the North, South, and Tuscany. Today, with her expanded world view, she continues to make her life an adventure.

So has Amber, who served four years in the U.S. Navy as the singer in the navy band. She then settled in Chicago where she met and married her life partner, Matthew. Today, she directs the music for a large church in the suburbs. She's also pursuing her dreams playing in a swing band called The Flat Cats.

CHANGING THE WORLD FEARLESSLY

How do you help a young girl become so sure of *who she is* that she can speak the truth wherever she goes? How do you instill a sense of justice and service in a whole generation?

So many middle-class, middle-aged people believe today's young people feel a sense of entitlement and are lazy and self-indulgent. I couldn't disagree more. I believe this generation of young women (and men) will change the world for the better. And because I've had the privilege of knowing three young women who fearlessly believe in themselves, I know that courage reigns and mind-killing fear can be conquered.

~ CHRISTIE WARD

This is a chapter from an upcoming book on raising the next generation of leaders. Christie Ward owns The Impact Institute, a training firm in Denver, Colorado. She facilitates Communication topics that make the difference for Sales results, productive Teams, and effective Leadership. In 2004 she won the ASTD Best Practices award for a program that lowered union grievances at AT&T in Denver 66%. She is past president of the ASTD-Rocky Mountain Chapter and on the board of the National Speakers Association of Colorado. She personally coached the World Champion of Public Speaking for the year 2000! Reach Christie at Christie@impactinst.com. Visit her at www.impactinst.com. Christie Ward © 2007

Re-Awakening to Love

I first saw him walking in my neighborhood. Intuitively, I felt there might be a connection but did not want to push it into happening before it was ready. One day we met at my mailbox. He was sitting on the grass with his back against the post playing the didgeridoo, an ancient Aboriginal instrument of hollowed out wood. Suddenly we were locked in an intense conversation that I can't remember now.

So began a gentle friendship of an older woman and a younger man having one thing in common—me from Australia and he appreciating the aboriginal culture from which I had come. We spoke of our experiences, sharing our thoughts and philosophies. And we began to listen deeply to discover what was important to us and the values we wished to embody. It was a sweet friendship that, for all our differences, showed we had much in common—both coming from a background of physical and emotional abuse, both having a commitment to transcend our conditioning and return to a state of love for all humankind.

Then, one day, it all changed. It was twilight when we decided to walk on the beach. The sun was cheerfully setting as we watched the children playing in the water, screams of pleasure echoing their laughter. Soon the families left, the sounds died down and we were alone on the beach with only the stars glistening and the waves gently lapping on the shore. He began to play his didgeridoo, this strange hollow limb of a tree, blowing into one end and placing the other end in my lap. Soon the primal sounds filled the air and the night was pulsing with anticipation. As he played, I began to tune into the energy produced by the didgeridoo; I found it arousing—sensual and sexual. My mind immediately told me this was wrong. I should not be feeling this but I couldn't block out the intensity of the vibration as it played out its primal sounds of passion. I surrendered, knowing I really had no choice.

Finally there came the all-enveloping silence and I returned from a place of excruciating pleasure to a state of embarrassment and confusion. How could I so easily be transported to another world by my young friend, transported to a world reserved for fantasies, not these physical sensations that threatened to overwhelm me?

Couldn't he see I was not the attractive twenty year old I had once been? I had aged, gained weight over the years, and had long put aside the thought that any man would be attracted to me. As I remained silent he looked at me, saying tenderly, "I see you and I appreciate all that is you!" How I had longed to hear these words. I have always wanted someone to look past the physical and see the beauty in me at my deepest level, and here was the recognition coming from someone half my age.

In the two years that followed, I found myself communicating through my body and emotions as I never had before, learning profound expressions of being in an intimate and loving relationship. Having dramatic sexual abuse as a child, over the years I had worked hard to integrate these experiences where I could now function in a healthy way. It took me a while to discover that I had found a partner who was willing to be my equal and go to the very depths of his emotional being. I was challenged to ask myself, was I really willing to let go of the subtle resentments and distrust that created a thin veil of unease between us? Underneath subtle put-downs and judgments, I found there was still hurt and fear of being hurt again. Our relationship became a place of intimate communion; a nurturing womb where we became naked in the true sense of the word, unveiling our vulnerable selves until there was no hidden wall of distrust or hurt between us.

I finally recognized that I could have a relationship that was more rewarding than I ever imagined. I just had to let go of how it looked and be in truth of what I was experiencing. How truly blessed I have been to experience the sacredness of this union and re-awaken to love.

~ SYDNEY SALT

Counsel, Workshop facilitator, www.DreamtimeCommunications.com © Copyright Sydney Salt. Reprinted with permission. Appeared in Visions Magazine, *February 2004*

Relationships

How lucky I am to have something that makes saying goodbye so hard.
~ FROM THE MOVIE *ANNIE*

Don't smother each other. No one can grow in the shade.
~ LEO BUSCAGLIA

Gift respect because you are a respectful person. Gift love because you are a loving person. The gift does not depend on the recipient's worthiness.
~ BETTY COLSTON

You cannot be lonely if you like the person you're alone with.
~ WAYNE W. DYER
Motivational speaker

The men in our lives are mirrors of what we believe about ourselves. So often we look to others to make us feel loved and connected when all they can do is mirror our own relationship with ourselves.
~ LOUISE L. HAY
Speaker, author of Empowering Women

People change and forget to tell each other.
~ LILLIAN HELLMAN

When the relationship is strong,
details rarely get in the way.
When the relationship is weak,
no amount of skilled negotiation
will bring about agreement.
~ DR. JIM HENNIG
Speaker, author, www.jimhennig.com

Relationships CONTINUED

I know for me the subject of how to be in a relationship is precious and complicated and challenging. It wouldn't be right to make it look too easy.

~ HELEN HUNT
Speaking about her approach to TV series Mad About You

Remember, we all stumble, every one of us. That's why it's a comfort to go hand in hand.

~ EMILY KIMBROUGH

Women, when seeking a long term partnership, take up a daily practice of writing, walking, or foot massage to feel a strong connection to your spiritual self. Feeding yourself will keep the fullness of your life vibrant!

~ JOANN MARINI
Relationship coach, author of Smart & Savvy Dater's Know . . .
www.MorethanAmour.com

Sometimes you have to get to know someone really well to realize you're really strangers.

~ MARY TYLER MOORE, ACTRESS

I see relationships that work and think to myself that's what I want. It's not that I am super picky about the male species, rather I am picky about making it work. I want 30 or more years out of one model. I am not one to trade in—or train a new one!!

~ BECKY PALMER
Age 52, never married

Relationships

Let us be grateful to people who make us happy, they are the charming gardeners who make our souls blossom.
~ MARCEL PROUST

Once the realization is accepted that even between the closest human beings infinite distances continue, a wonderful living side by side can grow, if they succeed in loving the distance between them which makes it possible for each to see the other whole against the sky.
~ RAINER MARIA RILKE

Trouble is part of your life, and if you don't share it, you don't give the person who loves you enough chance to love you enough.
~ DINAH SHORE

No road is long with good company.
~ TURKISH PROVERB

Shared joy is a double joy; shared sorrow is half a sorrow.
~ SWEDISH PROVERB

When two people truly love one another and set a common goal to honor one another and do whatever they can to help each other grow, expand and rise us to meet the best part of who they are, love will surely deepen and surpass all expectations.
~ CATHERINE TILLEY
Founder of the Institute for Global Healing and Publisher of WISE Publications
www.theglobalvoice.com

The five most essential words for a healthy, vital relationship are: "I apologize" and "you are right."
~ UNKNOWN

Relationships CONTINUED

If he says that you are too good for him—believe him.
~ UNKNOWN

Relationships are hard. It's like a full time job, and we should treat it like one. If your boyfriend or girlfriend wants to leave you, they should give you two week's notice. There should be severance pay, and before they leave you, they should have to find you a temp.
~ UNKNOWN, SUBMITTED BY MANDI NOWLIN

. . . we know more about the courtship and mating rituals of virtually every form of wildlife other than young men and women . . .
~ *WALL STREET JOURNAL*, AUGUST 3, 2001

We are not poor because the rich are rich. We are poor because we do not work with love.
~ MARIANNE WILLIAMSON
Author of A Return to Love

Don't settle for a relationship that won't let you be yourself.
~ OPRAH WINFREY

SECOND CHANCE—LOVE ANEW!

This is a love story . . .

It began in 1947! Years earlier, her father designed and drove one of the first electric cars to travel to the top of Mt. Wilson in Southern California, and before that, he had done some lighting work for Harry Houdini. Now, her father's business was specialty lighting and she was working in the front office, having recently graduated from college.

Then he walked through the door. He worked for RCA and was researching some new ideas for using fluorescent lighting. He was tall, well educated, and exactly where he needed to be . . . in more ways than one. When their eyes met . . . they both knew something special had happened. He began visiting the "shop" frequently, and it was only a matter of time before he bought her father's business, and asked for her hand in marriage.

Close friends from both families attended the wedding of James and Alys Alburger, among them, one of James' best friends, VJ Braun, and his wife. Their friendship continued for many years, although the two families would rarely see each other. At the time, their presence at the wedding had little significance. But the paths of life often take interesting turns.

Jim had purchased an acre of land in a remote part of Los Angeles known as La Canada with the intention of building a home for his new family. For the next 40 years Jim and Alys raised their 3 children, living in that custom-built home that never seemed to quite be finished. The love they shared during those years was revealed every time they went out—rarely seen not holding hands or "smooching."

In 1976, Jim was diagnosed with cancer, which eventually took his life in 1989.

Relarionships

But the love story doesn't end here . . .

In 1992, Alys received a completely unexpected telephone call from VJ. The love of his life, his wife Mary, had recently passed and, as VJ tells it, one evening he heard a voice that simply said "call Alys."

At first he ignored the voice, but it persisted until he finally made the call. Neither VJ nor Alys had any idea what would happen as a result of that first awkward meeting after so many years of not being in touch.

Neither of them was "looking," but over the next year or so, they each discovered a new love in their lives. When VJ "popped the question," Alys, at first reluctant, took only one day to say "yes."

The love between Alys and VJ was every bit as bright, if not brighter, than both of their first marriages. They were inseparable . . . always holding hands and "smooching"—Alys in her early 70s and VJ in his 80s.

The journey that led Alys and VJ to each other was a journey filled with love that was meant to be. It could never have been seen or predicted, and it could easily have been passed by. Fortunately, Alys and VJ both lived their lives knowing that love can sometimes be found in the most unexpected of places.

~ JAMES R. ALBURGER
Emmy award-winning voice-over talent, www.voiceacting.com

10 Ways to Improve Relationships—
Helping Bonds Thrive

1. The relationships you foster will become a mirror of the relationship you have with yourself. Francois de la Rochefoucauld said, "If we are incapable of finding peace in ourselves, it is pointless to search elsewhere." Learn to take responsibility for your own happiness and security and to treat yourself with acceptance, caring, and compassion.

2. Every person desires to be treated lovingly and simple kindness can often inspire kindness in return. Reflect on those who have made you feel most cared for and appreciated and emulate them in your interactions with others.

3. Though first impressions highlight similarities, it is often the differences between two people that make a relationship unique. Showing interest in the different cultures, beliefs, origins, and interests of your friends and loved ones can enrich and strengthen your ties.

4. Intimacy cannot thrive without contact. Making time for those close to you, even if it is simply writing a letter, demonstrates the depth of your feeling.

5. Positive thoughts and deeds inspire love, honesty, and respect. Negativity can only cause stress in relationships. Show others that you are grateful for the bounty with which you've been blessed and never hesitate to give to others.

Relationships CONTINUED

6. Share not only the laughter, but the tears as well. In doing so, you will become richer in spirit.

7. Conflict is a natural part of all relationships. Focusing on creating a balanced compromise rather than winning or losing an argument can draw you and your friend closer together.

8. Feelings of irritation, anger, or frustration flourish when we remain silent. Give voice to your emotions as they arise using neutral, non-accusatory statements. Make your feelings clear.

9. Being hurt by someone we care for is one of life's great sorrows, but forgiveness is one of life's great joys. Practicing forgiveness eases strain on relationships that have been put to the test and will bring peace to your soul.

10. Lillian Hellman said, "People change and forget to tell each other." We often don't know we've changed though we recognize and may be hurt by changes in others. Find the underlying qualities you appreciate in those you care for and be tolerant of their evolution for everything and everyone changes with time.

Romance

Need a little help or a few quick ideas on how to keep your romance alive? These spark up your love life!

Romance Rules to Live By

1. Laugh a lot, have a good sense of humor.
2. Look for new ways to fall in love all over again.
3. Let your love know you are there for them.
4. Show your partner you love them in every way possible.
5. Spend time apart, give each other space.
6. Add spice to your love life.
7. Avoid arguing.
8. Try new things.
9. Put feelings first.
10. Keep your relationship full of surprises.
11. Trust one another.
12. Believe romance is important to your relationship.
13. Have quality conversations with your partner.
14. Have faith in your relationship.
15. Tell your sweetheart how much they mean to you.
16. Be yourself.
17. Be romantic.
18. Always be there for each other.
19. Invest time shared together.
20. Whenever you have a misunderstanding talk about it together.
21. Treat your love as if they mean everything to you.
22. Treat your partner with the respect they deserve.
23. Never hang up the phone without saying I love you.
24. Never part without kissing.
25. Praise your partner often.

Romance <small>CONTINUED</small>

26. Never take your relationship for granted.
27. Make each moment with each other count.
28. Remember to take time for each other.
29. Keep happy.
30. Spoil your partner rotten!
31. Never go to sleep mad at each other.
32. Don't be afraid of making a fool of yourself.
33. Let your imagination be your guide.
34. Be a good listener.
35. Get to really know your partner.
36. Keep yourself trustworthy.
37. Never be predictable.
38. Be open and honest.
39. Keep open communication with your partner.
40. Maintain a great friendship with your love!

RITUALS OF LOVE

1. Take a few minutes each day to say I love you.
2. Start each day with a kiss and an "I love you."
3. End each day with a kiss and an "I love you."
4. Plan a monthly overnight/weekend getaway.
5. Take bubble baths together at least once a month.
6. Go out on at least one date a week.
7. Take walks together as often as possible.
8. Give your love a card once a week.
9. Set one day out of each week to do something special.
10. Say something sweet to your love every day.
11. Send an e-mail every day.
12. Every night before bed wish your partner sweet dreams.

ROMANTIC IDEAS

1. Give your partner a smile or soft kiss just let them know you are there for them.
2. Cuddle up together on the couch and watch a movie.
3. Cuddle up together and talk about your dreams and future plans.
4. Ask each other out on dates.
5. Write each other sweet love letters.
6. Send little gifts to them by surprise.
7. Call them up at work to remind them you love them.
8. Massage their feet and hands.
9. Place love notes in their lunch.
10. Buy their favorite cookies and hide them for your love.
11. Flirt with your sweetheart when you're in a store.
12. Blow an unexpected kiss.
13. Read to each other.
14. Get a babysitter.
15. Surprise your partner to a romantic weekend together.
16. Tell your love how sexy and beautiful they are.
17. Give special surprises like teddy bears with love notes attached.
18. Kiss in a lot of different ways.
19. Send a romantic e-card.
20. Stick little notes in their car.
21. Bring flowers when they least expect it.
22. Take showers together.
23. Picnic under moonlight.
24. Give a single perfect rose for no reason at all.
25. Dance on the balcony.
26. Try Tantric Loving.
27. Put on your favorite songs and dance around in the kitchen.
28. Create love, friendship and devotion pages for each other.

Romance

29. Write "I love you" on the bathroom mirror with soap or lipstick.
30. Have pizza with a love note delivered to your partners work.
31. Have coded messages to send notes to each other.
32. Go hiking.
33. Ride horses.
34. Cook together.
35. Light candles, drink wine with strawberries and have lots of loving!
36. Keep a mini mailbox, leave the flag up when you've left a love note.
37. Pretend like you're meeting for the first time.

~ EDITED BY ROMANCE STAFF, WWW.LOVINGYOU.COM

BARK, WIGGLE AND WAG!

The next time someone you love walks in the door, don't ask about what kind of a day they had. Just start wiggling, wagging, and jumping for joy.

Bark, whinny, honk, or quack, conveying how delighted you are to see them. Let your enthusiastic affection bubble over, and watch their reactions. Sure, at first they'll think you've lost your mind. Then they'll wonder what the heck you are up to. Finally, they'll laugh at you, with you, and for you. The best part is when they get into the routine and return your affection.

Allow yourself to receive their love. (If you have difficulty with this exercise, borrow a pet for a few days and allow the animal to teach you this fun and fond exercise in affection.)

~ CYNTHIA BRIAN
Speaker, author of the New York Times *best-selling* Chicken Soup for the Gardener's Soul, Be the Star You Are!, The Business of Show Business *and others. www.star-style.com*
Excerpt from Be the Star You Are! by Cynthia Brian
© Copyright Cynthia Brian. Reprinted with permission.

Self

What would you do to someone if they talked to your children the way you talk to yourself?

~ A QUESTION TO PONDER

Obstacles are the struggling emergence of our hidden inner desires seeking recognition.

~ PERRY A
Author of People Are Just Desserts, *www.PerryA.com*

There's a period of life when we swallow a knowledge of ourselves and it becomes either good or sour inside.

~ PEARL BAILEY

You never find yourself until you face the truth.

~ PEARL BAILEY

Love yourself first and everything else falls into line. You have to really love yourself to get anything done in this world.

~ LUCILLE BALL

You grow up the day you have your first real laugh, at yourself.

~ ETHEL BARRYMORE

When we learn to love ourselves, we are able to have a great deal of love for others.

~ LYDIA BOYD

The day I fell in love with myself was the day I truly started loving you. I didn't know it could be this wonderful.

~ SUBMITTED BY BRANDIE

Self CONTINUED

There is overwhelming evidence that the higher the level of self-esteem, the more likely one will be to treat others with respect, kindness, and generosity.
~ NATHANIEL BRANDEN

Self-esteem is the reputation we acquire with ourselves.
~ NATHANIEL BRANDEN

Let the world know you as you are, not as you think you should be . . .
~ FANNY BRICE

Your work is to discover your world and then with all your heart give yourself to it.
~ BUDDHA

You yourself, as much as anybody in the entire universe, deserve your love and affection.
~ BUDDHA

Love begins deep inside with self-love. We cannot get our self love outside, love cannot be created; it simply is a state of being. Remembering this is the key.
~ LINDA CAMMARATA, RN
International musician, www.LifeCoaching.net

When your heart speaks, take good notes.
~ JUDITH CAMPBELL

Take the time to come home to yourself every day.
~ ROBIN CASARJEAN

If there is light in the soul, there will be beauty in the person.
If there is beauty in the person, there will be harmony in the house.
If there is harmony is the house, there will be order in the nation.
If there is order in the nation, there will be peace in the world.

~ CHINESE PROVERB

When we let go of our investment in being a suffering victim, we let go of living in a world populated by enemies and victimizers, and we let go of an inner world of hate, recriminations, hopelessness and despair, accusations, blaming, and disempowerment. Then we can open ourselves up to a world of love, empowerment and abundance, free to hold open the space for that which is to reveal itself, in the inner knowledge that that which is can only be good, positive, loving, and for everyone's benefit.

~ JANE ILENE COHEN
Defining the New Paradigm, www.JaneCohen.net

And remember, no matter where you go, there you are.

~ CONFUCIUS

If you aren't good at loving yourself, you will have a difficult time loving anyone, since you'll resent the time and energy you give another person that you aren't even giving to yourself.

~ BARBARA DE ANGELIS

The willingness to accept responsibility for one's own life is the source from which self-respect springs.

~ JOAN DIDION

Self CONTINUED

The minute you settle for less than you deserve, you get even less than you settled for.

~ MAUREEN DOWD

Believe in yourself and what you feel. Your power will come from that.

~ MELISSA ETHERIDGE

The strongest single factor in prosperity consciousness is self-esteem: believing you can do it, believing you deserve it, believing you will get it.

~ JERRY GILLIES

In my day, we didn't have self-esteem, we had self-respect, and no more of it than we had earned.

~ JANE HADDAM

Never be afraid to sit awhile and think.

~ LORRAINE HANSBERRY
A Raisin in the Sun

There is an eternal landscape, a geography of the soul; we search for its outlines all our lives.

~ JOSEPHINE HART

There is nothing noble about being superior to other men. The true nobility is in being superior to your previous self.

~ HINDU PROVERB

Self CONTINUED

There's more than one answer to these questions
Pointing me in a crooked line.
And the less I seek my source for some definitive
The closer I am to fine.

~ INDIGO GIRLS
Song Lyrics to Closer to Fine

Life's lessons never end. A lesson is repeated until learned.

~ CATH KACHUR
Speaker, artist, www.HumanTuneUp.com

Love . . . when we love and accept ourselves, we shine. To shine, we must be true to ourselves whether it be in our choice of career, expressing our truth during a conflict, or taking care of ourselves. Self-love is the foundation of any sparkle we hope to create in this world. And when we love and accept ourselves, we create sparkle for all to see.

~ ANNMARIE LARDIERI
www.RelationshipRenaissance.com

Find yourself and you will find your true love. It's out there waiting, you just need to know how.

~ LUIS MARTINEZ

At this very moment, you may be saying to yourself that you have any number of admirable qualities. You are a loyal friend, a caring person, someone who is smart, dependable, fun to be around. That's wonderful, and I'm happy for you, but let me ask you this: are you being any of those things to yourself?

~ "DR. PHIL," PHILLIP C. MCGRAW
Author of The Ultimate Weight Solution: The 7 Keys to Weight Loss Freedom, *2003*

Self continued

There is only one great adventure and that is inward towards the self.

~ HENRY MILLER

I have low self-esteem, but I express it the healthy way . . . by eating a box of Double-Stuff Oreos.

~ CYNTHIA NIXON

I took a deep breath and listened to the old bray of my heart. I am. I am. I am.

~ SYLVIA PLATH

Love is an expression and assertion of self-esteem, a response to one's own values in the person of another. One gains a profoundly personal, selfish joy from the mere existence of the person one loves. It is one's own personal, selfish happiness that one seeks, earns, and derives from love.

~ AYN RAND
American writer and novelist

Self-esteem is only one of the factors that should be considered when we look to develop ourselves. Another factor is self-acceptance including loving ourselves, or at least not negatively judging ourselves, when we feel helpless, inferior and vulnerable. Self-esteem alone does not determine your ability to live your life fully. You are a unique human being. You should know what is good about you, accept your strengths and carry them with you into the world. Love who you are becoming.

~ MARCIA REYNOLDS
Speaker, author of Capture the Rapture: How to Step Out of Your Head and Leap Into Life

Be patient toward all that is unsolved in your heart and try to love the questions themselves like locked rooms and books that are written in a foreign tongue. Do not now seek the answers, which cannot be given you because you would not be able to live them. And the point is, to live everything. Live the questions now. Perhaps you will find them gradually, without noticing it, and live along some day into the answer.

~ RAINER MARIA RILKE
Letters to a Young Poet

No one can make you feel inferior without your consent.

~ ELEANOR ROOSEVELT
from This Is My Story, 1937

Work on bringing out a special trait that you admire about yourself and don't let anyone stop you from being like that.

~ MICHELLE C. ROUSH
Age 16, from an essay entitled To Be Free

Perfect is not what you try to be. Perfect is what YOU already ARE.

~ LAURA RUBINSTEIN
Coach, www.LBRandAssociates.com

There are chapters in every life which are seldom read and certainly not aloud.

~ CAROL SHIELDS

I have always regarded myself as the pillar of my life.

~ MERYL STREEP

We run away all the time to avoid coming face to face with ourselves.

~ UNKNOWN

Self CONTINUED

Sometimes the best way to figure out who you are is to get to that place where you don't have to be anything else.
~ UNKNOWN

Low self-esteem is like driving through life with your hand-break on.
~ UNKNOWN

Seek not good from without: seek it within yourselves, or you will never find it.
~ BERTHA VON SUTTNER

To establish true self-esteem we must concentrate on our successes and forget about the failures and the negatives in our lives.
~ DENIS WAITLEY
Motivational Speaker and author of self-help books

Self-esteem comes from walking through fear.
~ FRANCINE WARD, SPEAKER
Author of Esteemable Acts: 10 Actions for Building Real Self-Esteem

If you're willing to do the work, you will eventually become what I call a woman who is in full possession of herself.
~ OPRAH WINFREY

The whole point of being alive is to evolve into the complete person you were intended to be.
~ OPRAH WINFREY

Don't back down just to keep the peace. Standing up for your beliefs builds self-confidence and self-esteem.
~ OPRAH WINFREY

Sisters

What is a sister? She is your mirror shining back at you with a world of possibilities. She is your witness who sees you at your worst and best, and loves you anyway. She is your partner in crime, your midnight companion, someone who knows when you are smiling, even in the dark. She is your teacher, your defense attorney, your personal press agent, even your shrink.

Some days, she's the reason you wish you were an only child.

~ BARBARA ALPERT

I don't believe an accident of birth makes people sisters or brothers. It makes them siblings, gives them mutuality of parentage. Sisterhood and brotherhood is a condition people have to work at.

~ MAYA ANGELOU

No one knows better than a sister how we grew up, and who our friends, teachers, and favorite toys were. No one knows better than she.

~ DALE V. ATKINS

Sisters touch your heart in ways no other could. Sisters share . . . their hopes, their fears, their love, everything they have. Real friendship springs from their special bonds.

~ CARRIE BAGWELL

Sisters share the scent and smells-the feel of a common childhood.

~ PAM BROWN

Sisters CONTINUED

Loving a sister is an unconditional, narcissistic, and complicated devotion that approximates a mother's love . . . sisters are inescapably connected, shaped by the same two parents, the same trove of memory and experience.

~ MARY BRUNO
My Sister: A Treasury of Companionship

God Made Us Sisters, Prozac Made Us Friends.
~ BUMPER STICKER

Being in this band [the Spice Girls] is like having four (three now) older sisters. They all look after me and I couldn't dream of leaving them.

~ EMMA BUNTON
British singer

One's sister is a part of one's essential self, an eternal presence of one's heart and soul and memory.

~ SUSAN CAHILL

It is only the women whose eyes have been washed clear with tears who get the broad vision that makes them little sisters to all the world.

~ DOROTHY DIX
American journalist and columnist, 1870–1951

Siblings are the people we practice on, the people who teach us about fairness and cooperation and kindness and caring—quite often the hard way.

~ PAMELA DUGDALE

Sisters CONTINUED

Every sister has a fund of embarrassing stories she can bring out at the most effective moment.
~ PAMELA DUGDALE

Our sisters hold up our mirrors: our images of who we are and of who we can dare to become.
~ ELIZABETH FISHEL

We are sisters. We will always be sisters. Our differences may never go away, but neither, for me, will our song.
~ ELIZABETH FISHEL

A sister is both your mirror—and your opposite.
~ ELIZABETH FISHEL

A sister is a little bit of childhood that can never be lost.
~ MARION C. GARRETTY

I'm not the easiest person to live with. I'm kind of a slob. So for me to consider a roommate, it would have to be one of my sisters or something.
~ KATIE HOLMES
American actress

A sister is a gift to the heart, a friend to the spirit, a golden thread to the meaning of life.
~ ISADORA JAMES

Sisters

We are sisters. We will always be sisters. Our differences may never go away, but neither, for me, will our song.

~ NANCY KELTON
My Sister: A Treasury of Companionship

Having a sister is like having a best friend you can't get rid of. You know whatever you do, they'll still be there.

~ AMY LI

Sisters are connected throughout their lives by a special bond—whether they try to ignore it or not. For better or for worse, sisters remain sisters, until death do them part.

~ BRIGID MCCONVILLE
Author of Sisters: Love and Conflict Within The Lifelong Bond

Sisters is probably the most competitive relationship within the family, but once the sisters are grown, it becomes the strongest relationship.

~ MARGARET MEAD

There can be no situation in life in which the conversation of my dear sister will not administer some comfort to me.

~ LADY MARY WORLEY MONTAGU

A sister smiles when one tells one's stories—for she knows where the decoration has been added.

~ CHRIS MONTAIGNE

Sisters

A sister can be seen as someone who is both ourselves and very much not ourselves—a special kind of double.

~ TONI MORRISON

Beloved, you are my sister, you are my daughter, you are my face; you are me.

~ TONI MORRISON

To the outside world we all grow old. But not to brothers and sisters. We know each other as we always were. We know each other's hearts. We share private family jokes. We remember family feuds and secrets, family griefs and joys. We live outside the touch of time.

~ CLARA ORTEGA

She takes my hand and leads me along paths I would not have dared explore alone.

~ MAYA V. PATEL

Sisters function as safety nets in a chaotic world simply by being there for each other.

~ CAROL SALINE
From the TV series Sisters

What sets sisters apart from brothers and also from friends is a very intimate meshing of heart, soul and the mystical cords of memory.

~ CAROL SALINE
From the TV series Sisters

To have a loving relationship with a sister is not simply to have a buddy or confidante—it is to have a soulmate for life.

~ VICTORIA SECUNDA

Sisters CONTINUED

For when three sisters love each other with such sincere affection, the one does not experience sorrow, pain, or affliction of any kind, but the other's heart wishes to relieve, and vibrates in tenderness . . . like a well-organized musical instrument.

~ ELIZABETH SHAW

Husbands come and go; children come and eventually go. Friends grow up and move away. But the one thing that's never lost is your sister.

~ GAIL SHEENY
From the TV series Sisters

More than Santa Claus, your sister knows when you've been bad and good.

~ LINDA SUNSHINE

My sister taught me everything I need to know, and she was only in the sixth grade at the time.

~ LINDA SUNSHINE

My sisters are my memory, my therapy group, my mirrors, my cheer-leaders and mostly my friends.

~ TERRY SWEENEY

Together we look like our mother. Her same eyes, her same mouth, open in surprise to see, at last, her long-cherished wish.

~ AMY TAN

Only a sister can compare the sleek body that now exists with the chubby body hidden underneath. Only a sister knows about former pimples, failing math, and underwear kicked under the bed.

~ LAURA TRACY
From The Secret Between Us

I finally moved out of my parent's house. It was only fair to let my sister have her own room.

~ KATE WINSLET
British actress

TWIN SISTERS

Being a twin is very comforting as you always have someone with you who is your instant friend. My sister and I moved quite a bit when we were younger and we never had to worry about being alone, we always had each other and still do to this day. "Snuggled close, sharing secrets, running a muck—that was us—best friends forever." We laugh together, cry together, share each others success together. Being a twin is a gift that I cherish as few have the opportunity to have a friend for life.

~ JENNIFER TIBBOTT

Sons

THROUGH OUR EYES
To my dear son on the day of your birth
Evan Bryce O'Brien Gregory

I look into your eyes my son,
and this is what I see,
I see the things that are to come,
and how these things may be.

To you we give all we can,
in health, and wealth, and love,
so that when these things that are to come,
they may be as good can be.

Some things good and some things bad
are going to come your way,
but if you use the sight we have,
we will help to guide your way.

Mistakes in life, we've made a few,
and learned of how they hurt,
and if you listen to our hearts,
we'll guide you to a good start.

We try to guide you in our way,
and hope it helps you see;
There are so many good things in life,
and these we hope will be.

Sons CONTINUED

The road you take in life, my son,
is really up to you.
All your mom and I can do,
is guide you as you run.

One thing we ask of you my son,
is to be kind to everyone.
And if you have a chance to help someone,
then guide them as they run.

~ CHRIS GREGORY
© Copyright 1988. Reprinted with permission.

Sparkle-Tude Boosters

*T*oday, we need little attitude "boosters" to help us overcome negative thoughts and actions that so easily creep into our daily lives. We were born with passion, a natural zest for life, curiosity, playfulness and grace. These "Sparkle-Tudes" help us rejuvenate that unbridled excitement, spirit, and joyful expression:

1. Start off the day on a positive tone. How we wake up in the morning sets the pace for the rest of our day.

2. Have only positive thoughts toward yourself and others. Carefully guard your thoughts. Attitude, or our truest belief about things, is that highly powered magnet that either attracts—or repels! Life is composed of our moment-by-moment thoughts.

3. Look for the good in yourself and others. The Universal principle is that whatever thoughts we have about other people, these are also true of ourselves, as we are all connected, and we are all one. What we see in others are reflections of ourselves.

4. Believe in yourself, your talents, and your unique gifts. You were given significant strengths, and have developed skills to support those—use them!

5. Don't take things "personally." Let it go and move on!

6. Affirm a spirit of gratitude throughout the day. Start off the day with positive affirmations and anticipations of the day. I say, "Thank you God, for the gift of this glorious day. I rise, rejoice and am glad in it. Thank you for every way in which I experience your love. I give thanks that my every thought, word and act is only loving and supportive." End the day summarizing all the blessings you received.

7. Utilize these unconditional support systems to keep your balance, perspective and sanity: Pets; Faith; Passion Hobbies; and Special People.

~ SHERYL ROUSH
Speaker, author of Sparkle-Tudes!, Heart of A Woman, *and contributing author to* The Princess Principle: Women Helping Women Discover Their Royal Spirit, *18 inspirational stories, www.SparklePresentations.com*

Stay at Home Moms

You Can Have It All

1. *Make the most of your life experiences.* No matter what happens in your life, grow from those experiences. Don't allow difficult situations to diminish you or your dreams.

2. *Choose a primary focus for each stage of your life and be intensely committed to it.* A primary focus gives you a FRAME for the way you approach the world.

3. *No matter what your primary focus is, always make sure that you are in some way keeping your professional skills alive.* Read current writings in your field, rent tapes from the library, talk to others periodically who are still working full-time in your area of expertise, attend conferences and workshops, go back to school part time if you possibly can.

4. *Re-evaluate your priorities at least once a year, always keeping the long term in mind.* When the time is right to change priorities and focus, communicate that clearly to others and make decisions that support that change.

5. *Be creative.* Whatever your life situation may be, do the very best you can within the focus you've chosen.

6. *Network constantly.* Get to know people in your community, your church, schools. Let your skills and talents be known by others. Then, when your focus changes, you will already have a group of people who can recommend you.

Stay at Home Moms CONTINUED

7. *Believe in yourself and your dreams.* Even though you may have chosen to put your career "on the back burner" for a while, always approach each life task or experience like a professional.

~ BARBARA A. GLANZ
Consultant, Work/Life Balance Expert, author of CARE Packages for the Home—Dozens of Ways to Regenerate Spirit Where You Live *and* Balancing Acts: More Than 250 Guilt-free, Creative Ideas to Blend your Work and your Life, *www.BarbaraGlanz.com*

As a stay at home mom I feel it is important for other stay at home moms to remember that our children are only young once. The investment in their lives that we get to make as stay at home moms is priceless. There is no higher calling than being available for our children. To love our children and to nurture them is a real blessing.

~ MARY J. MCMAHON

Teenagers

Never lend your car to anyone to whom you have given birth.
~ ERMA BOMBECK

The young always have the same problem—how to rebel and conform at the same time. They have now solved this by defying their parents and copying one another.
~ QUENTIN CRISP

Few things are more satisfying than seeing your children have teenagers of their own.
~ DOUG LARSON

The best way to keep children at home is to make the home atmosphere pleasant, and let the air out of the tires.
~ DOROTHY PARKER

Heredity is what sets the parents of a teenager wondering about each other.
~ LAURENCE J. PETER

Teenagers complain there's nothing to do, then stay out all night doing it.
~ BOB PHILLIPS

Adolescence is perhaps nature's way of preparing parents to welcome the empty nest.
~ KAREN SAVAGE AND PATRICIA ADAMS
Authors of The Good Stepmother: A Survival Guide

The average teenager still has all the faults his parents outgrew.
~ UNKNOWN

Trust

If you want more of something—you need to give it first.

If you want more recognition—you need to recognize others first.

If you want others to trust you—you need to trust them first.

If you want others to love you—you need to love them first.

~ SHERYL ROUSH
Speaker, author of Sparkle-Tudes! *and* Heart of A Mother, *www.SparklePresentations.com*

BREATH OF GOD

I had decided to go to Detroit to visit with my Grandparents without my parents staying there. Maybe I was 9 or 10 years old when this happened. At least it was in an era when kids could travel alone; I went by train, the New York Central. After a few days, I became homesick for my parents and my own room and bed. I was crying as I tried to go to sleep, but just could not keep thinking about how I was all alone in a big city away from my Mom and Dad. My Grandmother heard me crying and she came in my room asking if I was sick or having pain. I told her I felt, all alone and scared.

She asked me if I believed in God. I told her that I suppose so, but that right now I was more frightened to be alone, away from my own home. She told me that God was with me all the time, no matter where I was. I asked her how that could be so. She explained that like the air and wind, God was everywhere even if we could not see God. She told me to take a big breath and when I did, she told me that God was inside me every time I take a breath of air and that I was never alone, even if I never had any brothers or sisters or anybody, ever.

Trust CONTINUED

I thought about what she said and told her that I wanted to try it out, feeling like God was with me even if no one else was there.

She told me a little prayer, turned out the light and left the room. I felt OK after she went to her bed and slept all night. The next morning, I told her that it was okay for me to stay in Detroit as long as we had planned and that I did not need to be scared again.

I share this story with you because as an adult, there have been times now when I felt scared like the child I was then. I do remember to breathe in and out, very deeply, and this reminds me of God and how I can regain my courage to overcome many fears and tragedies. Physically, it calms my body and mind to be able to think how to overcome the loss of energy it takes to move in a positive direction when the dark side of life has pulled me down.

~ BLANCHE KATZ, MSN, RN, C.S., GNP

Unconditional Support

4 Simple Ways to Nurture Yourself
and Keep Your Sanity

*H*ere are four ways to help keep balance in your daily life, so you are able to be there for yourself, your children, and loved ones. According to stress management experts, we have four support systems available that offer us unconditional love and support.

Pets Pets are nonjudgmental, forgiving, sensitive and supportive. They instinctively KNOW when we need a hug or are feeling emotional, depressed and upset, and don't run at the first sign of tears! Medical research even proves that hugging a pet lowers blood pressure, and helps to rebuild the immune system.

Faith Spiritual Belief System This inner compass enables us bring forth that wisdom, authenticity and insight into all we do on a daily basis. These beliefs center our moral foundation, offering direction, and trust to walk to our path in this world.

Passion Hobbies Passion Hobbies are pastimes that nurture our spirit and balance our lives. Reading; walking, dancing, running, aerobics or exercise; crafts; puzzles; playing with kids; or shopping!

Special People These may be relatives, or significant others, still be living, or have already made their transition. Highly supportive kindred spirits. We can pick up conversations with them, right where we left off, without missing a beat.

You have numerous gifts to give to the world today— and those gifts are needed. Nurture yourself first, and those challenges become easier to handle, with less stress, greater peace and calm. Utilize these unconditional support systems to bring you more balance and joy in your daily life.

~ SHERYL ROUSH
Speaker, author of Sparkle-Tudes! *and* Heart of A Mother, *www.SparklePresentations.com*

Women

TOP TEN THINGS ONLY WOMEN UNDERSTAND:

10. Cat's facial expressions.
9. The need for the same style of shoes in different colors.
8. Why bean sprouts aren't just weeds.
7. "Fat" clothes.
6. Taking a car trip without trying to beat your best time.
5. The difference between beige, ecru, cream, off-white, and eggshell.
4. Cutting your bangs to make them grow.
3. Eyelash curlers.
2. The inaccuracy of every bathroom scale ever made.
   and the Number One thing only women understand:
1. OTHER WOMEN

One is not born a woman, one becomes one.
~ SIMONE DE BEAUVOIR

Real women don't have hot flashes. They have power surges.
~ CHRISTINE MANSFIELD

Oprah Winfrey interviewed Dolly Parton and asked if the size of her breasts were ever an issue. "These? I call these my massive distraction."

I am Woman, hear me roar!
~ HELEN REDDY

Born a precious child, our Life beckons to find the wise woman inside, only to show us the truth about our lives is to remain that precious child, after all.

~ SHERYL ROUSH
Speaker, author of Sparkle-Tudes! *and* Heart of A Mother, *www.SparklePresentations.com*

Women in History

*T*he history books are filled with hundreds of stories praising men of honor and valor who changed the course of his-story, and in comparison, there are just a handful of women mentioned who have made a difference.

In searching the archives for women who have valiantly spoken up and changed the course of history equal to the likes of Abraham Lincoln, Thomas Edison and Martin Luther King, I polled both men and women, "Name four men who radically changed history." Four names immediately came forth without hesitation. "That was too easy!" Then I asked, "Now, name four women who have equally changed history." "Wow, that's a hard one."

Everyone knows that Edison invented the electric light bulb; Alexander Graham Bell, the telephone; Henry Ford, the first automobile; and the Wright Brothers were the first to take to the friendly skies, right? Now, stop and take a moment to name three things invented by women. How did you do?

When it comes to creating, women have come up with some amazing ideas that come from the heart such as:

The Paper Bag—Margaret Knight, 1861
Margaret received her first patent when she was 30, for a machine that cut, pasted and glued paper bags together. Even then she had to fight in court with a man who tried to steal her idea by stating that a mere woman didn't have the sense to invent such a machine. She won her case and went on to patent over 22 inventions.

Radium and Polonium Used in X-rays—Madam Marie Curie, 1887
Marie discovered the two radioactive elements, radium and polonium. She became the most famous woman in the world by the end of World War I, and in 1911, she won the first of two Nobel prizes.

Women in History

The Dishwasher—Josephine Cochran, 1893

In 1886, Josephine proclaimed in disgust, "If nobody else is going to invent a dishwashing machine, I'll do it myself!" So she did, and founded a company that eventually became KitchenAid. Unfortunately for her, the dishwasher didn't catch on until the 1950s.

The Windshield Wiper—Mary Anderson, 1903

Mary received her first patent for a window cleaning device in 1903. By 1916, her invention was standard equipment on all American cars.

Satellite Communications—Hedy Lamar, 1941

For all of us over forty, the name Hedy Lamar may ring a bell. She was a movie star "pin-up girl" in the 1940s. She had both beauty and brains. The original purpose for her invention was to guide torpedoes by radio signal during World War II. She received a patent for her idea in 1941. When the patent expired, Sylvania modified it slightly and used her Secret Communications System for satellite technology.

Scotchguard—Patsy Sherman, 1952

Patsy, a research chemist at 3M, discovered Scotchguard when a glass bottle containing a batch of latex mixture was accidentally dropped on an assistant's canvas shoe. She was inducted into the National Inventors Hall of Fame in 1983.

Liquid Paper—Bette Nesmith Graham, 1956

Originally called "mistake out," this handy invention came out of the need to cover up the mistakes of a secretary. Using art materials in her kitchen, Bette created a product that every secretary in her building wanted to buy. With her nine-year-old son, Michael Nesmith, she bottled and filled orders. By 1967, these humble mother and son

Women in History

beginnings had grown into a million dollar business. In 1980, Bette sold the business for $47.5 million and died six months later. Oh, by the way, if the name Michael Nesmith sounds familiar, it's because he is one of the original members of The Monkees, a popular 70s singing group. "Here they come . . . ."

◆ ◆ ◆

Before the 1840s, women were not even allowed to hold a patent in their own name, so all of the inventions created by women had to be filed with a man's name. He, of course, got the credit and his own chapter in his-story. I wonder how many of the inventions we use today were invented by women and hidden under the assumed name of a man in order to obtain a legal patent?

Could it be that Mrs. Graham Bell or Mrs. Thomas Edison had their feminine fingers somewhere in those two creations? We may never know, but it's kind of fun to think about it. At present, statistics show that 20 percent of all inventions are from the creative minds of women, and the number is projected to reach 50 percent over the next generation. "You go, girl!"

~ JONI WILSON

Speaker, singer, voice expert, authorJoniWilsonVoice.com © 2005 Joni Wilson. All Rights Reserved. Reprinted with Permission. From Thunder Behind the Silence: When a Woman Finds Her Voice

Worthiness

Ask for what you want and be prepared to get it.

~ MAYA ANGELOU
American poet, writer, and actress

. . . to be loved, happy, not to settle for something less than you deserve.

~ JENNIFER ANISTON

You yourself, as much as anybody in the entire universe, deserve your love and affection.

~ BUDDHA

I had to admit that my "perfect" childhood left me with hurts, disappointments and blocks that needed to be healed. I had to admit that this individual who pretended to have it all together was really a frightened little girl who wanted someone to tell her that she was lovable even if she wasn't perfect. I came to learn that this message needed to come from me.

~ COLETTE CARLSON
Speaker, contributing author of Conversations on Success

No matter what age you are, or what your circumstances might be, you are special, and you still have something unique to offer. Your life, because of who you are, has meaning.

~ BARBARA DE ANGELIS

Worthiness

Living with integrity means:

- *Not settling for less than what you know you deserve in your relationships.*
- *Asking for what you want and need from others.*
- *Speaking your truth, even though it might create conflict or tension.*
- *Behaving in ways that are in harmony with your personal values.*
- *Making choices based on what you believe, and not what others believe.*

~ BARBARA DE ANGELIS

When I was a teenager, I recall struggling with my identity and my self-worth. There were many times that I came home and cried on my bed. Boys made fun of me, and called me names. There were numerous times I felt ugly and worthless. I will never forget the gift of you! The beautiful words you shared with me. You kept telling me not to pay attention to such nonsense, and how beautiful and special I was. You forever gave me strength, love, courage and passion. Your support and love are in my heart forever. I love forever, with every fiber of my being.

~ LISA R. DELMAN
Speaker, author of Letters from the Heart, To My Mother: A Daughter's Voice
www.HeartfeltMatters.com

Inner self-worth and self-esteem are the most important things a woman can possess . . . When our self-worth is strong, we will not accept positions of inferiority and abuse.

~ LOUISE L. HAY, SPEAKER
Author of Empowering Women

Worthiness CONTINUED

A person's worth is contingent upon who he is, not upon what he does, or how much he has. The worth of a person, or a thing, or an idea, is in being, not in doing, not in having.

~ ALICE MARY HILTON

Love . . . when we love and accept ourselves, we shine. To shine, we must be true to ourselves whether it be in our choice of career, expressing our truth during a conflict, or taking care of ourselves. Self-love is the foundation of any sparkle we hope to create in this world. And when we love and accept ourselves, we create sparkle for all to see.

~ ANNMARIE LARDIERI
www.RelationshipRenaissance.com

Each one of us has a contribution to make and a legacy to leave. We all have at least one person who needs what we have to offer. How easily we forget this in the middle of a busy day or a personal crisis. How much we need to remember this! You are precious, unrepeatable gift to the world. Unwrap yourself. The world is waiting for you.

~ MARY MARCDANTE
Speaker, author of Living with Enthusiasm: How the 21-Day Smile Diet Can Change Your Life

Your Being is an unfathomable mystery of wonder and beauty. Turn your gaze inward and see what is there. Then, honor that Being.

~ PEGGY O'NEILL
Speaker, author of Walking Tall: Overcoming Inner Smallness No Matter What Size You Are, *www.YoPeggy.com*

You demonstrate your values and beliefs daily by the way you live your life.

~ LYNN PIERCE
Author of Change One Thing, Change Your Life, *www.ChangeOneThing.com*

Worthiness continued

If you don't set a baseline standard for what you'll accept in life, you'll find it's easy to slip into behaviors and attitudes or a quality of life that's far below what you deserve.

~ ANTHONY ROBBINS
Professional communicator, advisor to leaders

Remember always that you have not only a right to be an individual, you have an obligation to be one. You cannot make any useful contribution in life unless you do this.

~ ELEANOR ROOSEVELT

Reflect your brilliance!

~ SHERYL ROUSH
Speaker, author of Sparkle-Tudes! *and* Heart of A Mother, *www.SparklePresentations.com*

What is important is simple: Know what you value and invest your time accordingly. This is integrity and it will bring you peace.

~ RHOBERTA SHALER, PHD
www.OptimizeLifeNow.com

We can tell our values by looking at our checkbook stubs.

~ GLORIA STEINEM

The God that gives us life gives us the tools for our expansion and is not responsible for how we use those tools.

~ JONI WILSON
Speaker, singer, voice expert, authorJoniWilsonVoice.com © 2005 Joni Wilson. All Rights Reserved. Reprinted with Permission. From Thunder Behind the Silence: When a Woman Finds Her Voice

You don't get what you deserve.
You get what you *think* you deserve.

~ OPRAH WINFREY

SHERYL ROUSH

*S*parkle-Tude™ Expert Sheryl Roush presents inspirational programs that rekindle the spirit, raise the bar, and create excitement.

Humorous, creative and authentic, she relates real-life experiences in a positive, lighthearted way that enriches the soul. She playfully engages audiences, offering valuable how-to tips while entertaining with stories, songs and surprises. Audiences "experience" her presentations—with lasting feelings, results, and significance.

Participants throughout Australia, Canada, England, Malaysia, Northern Ireland, Puerto Rico, Singapore, and the US have awarded her top-ratings for content, interaction and delivery style.

She was only the third woman in the world to earn the elite status of Accredited Speaker as honored by Toastmasters International (now in 93 countries) for outstanding platform speaking and professionalism. Sheryl was crowned "Ms. Heart of San Diego" for 2004 and 2005, and "Reina de La Esperanza" 2007 (Queen of Hope) for contributions to the community.

Sheryl has presented on programs alongside celebrities including: Olivia Newton-John, Jane Seymour, Art Linkletter, Thurl Bailey, *Good Morning America's* Joan Lunden, *Men are from Mars* author John Gray, *Chicken Soup for the Soul* co-author Mark Victor Hansen, *One-minute Millionaire's* Robert G. Allen, and keynote closed for *Commander in Chief's* Geena Davis.

Have Sheryl present an energizing keynote opening—or wrap-up sensational closing—for your event!

Highly-customized workshops, special events and retreat facilitation.

Sparkle Presentations
Sheryl@SparklePresentations.com
www.SparklePresentations.com
Call Toll Free (800) 932-0973 to schedule!

Are low morale, high-stress and poor attitudes affecting your customer service, productivity and teamwork today?

Need to rekindle the spirit on your organization?

Bring in the Sparkle-Tude™ Expert to energize positive trends!

PROGRAMS INCLUDE:

Sparkle-Tude!™ Keeping a Sparkling Attitude Every Day
- Discover 7 Sparkle-Tude™ Boosters for home, work and life
- Learn how to deal with difficult people and challenging situations
- Enjoy 67 ways to stay sane and lighthearted in stressful times

Creating a Positive Work Environment
Tips and ideas to bring positive attitudes, connection and spirit to work. Morale-boosting team communication tactics and cooperation!

Customer Service with Heart
Enhanced interpersonal, communication and sales skills with attitude-boosters to generate authentic and exceptional service.

Heart of A Woman *and* Heart of a Mother *presentations*
Celebrations and tributes to amazing women

Audiences include:

7-Up
Abbott Laboratories
AT&T
Baptist Memorial Health
　Care Corp.
Bucknell University—
　Small Business Dev.
Central California Women's
　Conferences
ChildStart
Columbus Chamber of
　Commerce Women's Day
County of Los Angeles
Ernst & Young
GlaxoSmithKline
Hong Kong Baptist
　University

IBM
Institute of Real Estate
　Management
Intuit/Turbo Tax
Kaiser Permanente
　Physician Recruiters
Kiddie Academy
Latham & Watkins,
　int'l law firm
Los Angeles Unified
　Schools (120 programs)
McMillin Realty
Mitsubishi
Phillips Morris of Asia,
　Hong Kong
San Diego Zoo
Sharp Healthcare

Sheraton
Singapore Press
Sony
Stampin' Up!
　direct sales
UC-Berkeley
Union Bank
US Census Bureau
Verizon Wireless
Westin Hotels
Women in Business
　Symposium
Women's Council
　of Realtors